The Worshiping Body

The Worshiping Body

The Art of Leading Worship

KIMBERLY BRACKEN LONG

WESTMINSTER
JOHN KNOX PRESS
LOUISVILLE · KENTUCKY

© 2009 Kimberly Bracken Long

First edition
Published by Westminster John Knox Press
Louisville, Kentucky

09 10 11 12 13 14 15 16 17 18—10 9 8 7 6 5 4 3 2 1

Scripture quotations from the New Revised Standard Version of the Bible are copyright © 1989 by the Division of Christian Education of the National Council of the Churches of Christ in the U.S.A. and are used by permission.

Excerpt from Church of Scotland, *Common Order* (Edinburgh: St. Andrews Press, 1994). Used by permission. Excerpt from Eugenia Gable, "Among the Ribbons," *Call to Worship: Liturgy, Music, Preaching, and the Arts* 42.3 (February 2009). Used by permission. Excerpt from Scott Haldemann, "Washed and Ready: Baptism as Call and Gift of Ministry," *Call to Worship: Liturgy, Music, Preaching, and the Arts* 40.2 (2006). Used by permission. Excerpt from International Commission on English in the Liturgy, *Opening Prayers: Collects in Contemporary Language, Scripture-Related Prayers for Sundays and Holy Days, Years A, B, & C* (Norwich: Canterbury Press, 2001). Used by permission of Canterbury Press and Westminster John Knox Press. All rights reserved. Excerpt from Mark Searle, "Bowing," *Assembly* 6.3 (1979), 79; quoted in Kathleen Hughes, R.S.C.J., *Lay Presiding: The Art of Leading Prayer* (Collegeville, Minnesota: The Liturgical Press, 1988). Used by permission of the Center for Liturgy. All rights reserved. Excerpt from "What Is This Place?" Text by Huub Oosterhuis, translated by David Smith, in *Evangelical Lutheran Worship* (Minneapolis: Augsburg Fortress, 2006). © 1967, Gooi en Sticht, BV., Baarn, The Netherlands. All rights reserved. Exclusive agent for English-language countries: OCP Publications, 5536 NE Hassalo, Portland, OR 97213. All rights reserved. Used with permission.

Some of the material in this book has appeared in various periodicals and is reprinted here by permission of the editor of each journal. A version of chapter 1 appeared as "Speaking Grace, Making Space: The Art of Worship Leadership" in *Journal of Religious Leadership* (Spring 2008): 35–52. A segment of chapter 3 was originally part of a lecture titled "In from the Street: When Homeless Christians Join the Worshiping Assembly," delivered at the Seattle Institute for Liturgy and Worship in 2006 and at Columbia Theological Seminary in 2007; this lecture subsequently was published in *Journal for Preachers* 31, no. 3 (Easter 2008): 31–40. A portion of the segment on the benediction in chapter 4 appeared in "May the Lord Bless You and Keep You: Liturgy as the Locus of Blessing," published in *Call to Worship: Liturgy, Music, Preaching, and the Arts* 38.4 (May 2005): 3–9. The section on gestures in eucharistic prayer that is part of chapter 5 first appeared in *Reformed Worship* 23 (88), June 2008, as "'The Lord Be with You': The Language of Gesture in Eucharistic Prayer." A brief excerpt in chapter 6 was originally published in an editorial for *Call to Worship: Liturgy, Music, Preaching, and the Arts.*

Book design by Sharon Adams
Cover design by Pam Poll Design
Cover photo: GregSchneider.com

Library of Congress Cataloging-in-Publication Data

Long, Kimberly Bracken.
  The worshiping body : the art of leading worship / Kimberly Bracken Long.
    p. cm.
  ISBN 978-0-664-23311-2 (alk. paper)
  1. Public worship. 2. Body, Human—Religious aspects—Christianity. I. Title.
  BV15.L65 2009
  264—dc22

                                                            2009008878

PRINTED IN THE UNITED STATES OF AMERICA

♾ The paper used in this publication meets the minimum requirements of the American National Standard for Information Sciences—Permanence of Paper for Printed Library Materials, ANSI Z39.48-1992

Westminster John Knox Press advocates the responsible use of our natural resources. The text paper of this book is made from 30% post-consumer waste.

For Nathan and Daniel,
lights of my life

Contents

Acknowledgments

No book comes to life in a vacuum, and I am grateful to so many friends and colleagues who have thought through these questions over the years. Ron Byars, David Gambrell, Martha Moore-Keish, Kathleen O'Connor, and Christine Yoder read drafts of various chapters and offered valuable advice. Members of the Liturgical Language Seminar of the North American Academy of Liturgy read an early draft of chapter 4, providing helpful critique. Melanie Shaw read the complete manuscript in the midst of her own teaching and studying, pointing out gaps and asking helpful questions all along the way. Adam Copeland gave invaluable help with final editorial details. Most important to the process are the students at Columbia Theological Seminary in Decatur, Georgia, who worked through this material with me in classrooms and chapels, especially Clyde Bearss, Stephane Cobbert, Wendy Dewberry, David Hawkins, Sharon Junn, Andrew Kim, Daniel McCurdy, Katherine Miller, Marcel van Bulck, Robin Williamson, and James Yao.

Most of all, I am indebted to my family, my constant companions in working out just what it is that makes for passionate and faithful presiding: my sons, Nathan Price and Daniel Price, who know beauty, authenticity, and theological integrity when they see it; my parents, Peggie and Donald Bracken, who raised me to love the worshiping community of faith and have given excellent gifts of preaching, prayer, and song to so many; and my beloved husband, Tom, whose loving heart, irrepressible spirit, and incisive mind have enriched my life and work beyond measure.

Chapter 1

Called Out from the Body

*E*very Sunday morning, people make their way to churches in hopes that something significant will happen. Hungering for an encounter with the holy, they come, but often they leave disappointed. There might be any number of reasons for this—they were distracted, or the sermon fell flat, or the music failed to soar. Or perhaps God simply was silent.

One could name many more reasons why worship can seem lifeless, but sometimes the problem lies with those of us who lead worship. We are confused about who we are supposed to be, what we are supposed to do, and how we are supposed to relate to the congregation. Sometimes we pray as though we do not really believe anyone is listening and address the creator of the cosmos in the same cadences we use to talk about football or recipes. We jog around the sanctuary with a microphone and call it preaching, without seeming to notice that the burden of proclaiming the gospel is a holy and frightening thing. Or we enter the pulpit "depending on the Spirit," after doing little praying and less studying or contemplating, expecting that whatever happens to tumble out of our ill-prepared mouths will be a "word from the Lord." Maybe those of us who are cantors or song leaders are more intent on impressing listeners with our voices than on expressing the text and tone of the music. The truth of the matter is, few of us who lead worship have thought about, or have been taught about, how our voices, bodies, and spirits affect the ethos of worship. We study preaching, pastoral care, and education in seminary, but few of us have the opportunity to study the history, theology, and practice of worship. Musicians are often schooled as performers but receive little guidance in theological or pastoral matters. And church members, while given responsibilities for leading worship, rarely receive training for their tasks.

Probing into the whys and hows of liturgical leadership—not just what to do, but also the theology and spirituality that underlie the practical techniques

1

and skills—is a complicated endeavor. Learning to lead worship is challenging because so much about being a good leader of worship is difficult to describe. Certainly there are things to say about the proper use of the voice and evocative gestures and appropriate words, but much of what lies at the heart of the matter is less about correctness and more about passion.

Furthermore, we're not sure how to imagine ourselves in the role of worship leader. Who are we when we lead worship? Are we priests representing the people before God, preachers proclaiming the truth of the Gospels, pastors caring for the needs of the flock, or worship enliveners making sure the people are engaged? There is a bit of truth in all these labels, but none of them is sufficient. Since Justin Martyr used the term in the second century, some have called worship leaders "presiders"—people called out from the midst of a community of believers to ensure that the Word is proclaimed and the Sacraments enacted. That name serves our purposes well, because it describes those who are all at once priests, preachers, pastors, and worship enliveners, whose calling is to faithfully lead a worshiping assembly in its encounter with the one, triune, holy God who meets us in Scripture and preaching; in water, bread, and wine; in singing and praying; in almsgiving; in gathering and sending.

To focus on what presiders do, and how they do it, is tricky business, because such a focus implies that the one who leads is the star of the show. This, of course, is far from the truth. Gordon Lathrop reminds us that there would be no presiders without the people gathered for worship, and no people without the Word.[1] And yet, as Calvin firmly believed, the worshiping community needs one of its own to be called out to proclaim God's Word through all the means of grace—preaching, baptism, and the Lord's Supper—not for the sake of the presider's status or honor, but for the sake of the people. In considering the theology, spirituality, and practice of presiding, we hold in blessed tension two truths: that those who preside are *called out* from the body for a particular ministry, and that their chief end is to *serve* that same body. In other words, it is the body—the congregation, the assembly, the worshipers—who are the real focus of this book.

A second complication lies in the fact that, while it is indisputable that there are presiders who carry out their tasks with great skill and depth, excellence in presiding is not a goal in and of itself. There are presiders who never seem to miss a beat, whose pronunciation and intonation are perfectly executed, who seem to say all the right words and perform all the right gestures. And yet something is still missing—some inclination of mystery, perhaps, or of deep joy. Or maybe we long for the sense that this person leading the prayers really does imagine that we dare to speak in the presence of God, and marvels with us: Who are we, that you care for us . . . ? (Ps. 8:4). Sometimes what makes for great theater does not make for great worship.

If excellence is presiding is not the chief concern, then, what is? "Effective" presiding is the goal—that is, faithful leadership that most fully evokes the people's worship. To be sure, certain skills and techniques make for good worship leadership; yet the underlying, and most important, discussion is about the spirituality of it all. This, of course, is what makes the task of writing about presiding so difficult, because so much of it is about what cannot be seen—it is about spirit and flame, obedience and abandon, speech and silence, the embodiment of that which cannot be seen. And yet it is a task we must undertake, for this calling to lead God's people in worship demands the faithful devotion of all that we have—body, mind, and spirit.

It might seem that a book about presiding would be addressed to those Christians who are ordained to the ministry of Word and Sacrament, but much of this discussion speaks to all people who have a part in leading worship— musicians, elders, deacons, lectors, dancers, and artists. Certainly questions of ordained ministry come into play; yet the discussions surrounding how we understand ordination as well as the nature of liturgical leadership inform the whole church, and therefore a wide range of folks who are engaged in leading worship.

It is impossible to write a one-size-fits-all book on presiding in the current North American context, in which a wide range of liturgical expressions exist side by side. What speaks to an Episcopal priest in a parish committed to the Anglican tradition may not seem so relevant to a worship leader in a praise and worship service, and the concerns of the minister of an emergent urban house church might seem, on the surface, to have little to do with those of the pastor of a Presbyterian suburban congregation. Yet underneath our differences in style and expression, there are theological convictions about who we are as worship leaders—and how to be most faithful in that work—that we hold in common.

To be sure, an author's own context necessarily shapes her assumptions and convictions about worship; even vocabulary marks an author as being from one corner of the church or another. It will be clear to readers that I write from a Reformed theological framework, and that I have been informed by leaders of the liturgical renewal movement in North America. I hope that it will be equally clear that I harbor not only a deep appreciation for the ancient traditions of the church, but also a keen desire to help shape new and vital ways of worshiping in the twenty-first century.

Called Out from the Body

"What do you need in order to have *church*?"[2] Depending on who you are and what worship tradition or style you come from, you may answer this in different ways. Some might say that you can't "have church" without a stirring word from the Lord. Some would say that you've got to go to God in prayer. Others would insist on the Eucharist as the defining feature of "having church." Some would require silence, while others would insist on joyful, praise-filled singing. Those are all good answers; but the one thing that every tradition or style has in common is people. Not only is worship impossible without people to do it, but there would be no need for worship leaders without worshipers. To put it in the theological parlance of one scholar, the gathered congregation, or assembly, is "the most basic symbol of Christian worship."[3]

One could argue that we need other things, too. Calvin insisted that the church is not the church without two essential marks: "Whenever we see the Word of God purely preached and heard, and the sacraments administered according to Christ's institution, there, it is not to be doubted, a church of God exists [cf. Eph. 2:20]." Undergirding that statement, however, is the assumption of a gathered community, for he continues, "For his promise cannot fail: 'Wherever two or three are gathered in my name, there I am in the midst of them' [Matt. 18:20]."[4] It is the people who are essential to worship, and as the gathered assembly they have symbolic significance, as do the Bible and pulpit, the water and font or baptistry, and the bread and wine and table.

It has been true ever since the earliest days of the church: when Christians gather for worship, they gather to *do* something. After the Spirit stirred three thousand new believers to be baptized through Peter's Pentecost sermon, "they devoted themselves to the apostles' teaching and fellowship, to the breaking of bread and the prayers" (Acts 2:42). In other words they proclaimed the gospel to one another, shared the Lord's Supper, and prayed together. We recognize this pattern, of course, because it is our own. We are initiated into the body of Christ—the priesthood of all believers—through baptism. When we gather as the body, we take part in preaching, the meal, fellowship, prayer, and giving gifts for the poor.

Not only is baptism our initiation into the body; it is also our ordination to ministry—that is, to our Christian vocation. We believe, with Paul, that all of us are given charisms, gifts of the Spirit, for the common good.

> Now there are varieties of gifts, but the same Spirit; and there are varieties
> of services, but the same Lord; and there are varieties of activities, but it is

the same God who activates all of them in everyone. To each is given the manifestation of the Spirit for the common good. (1 Cor. 12:4–7)

Wisdom, knowledge, faith, healing miracles, prophecy, discernment of spirits, tongues, the interpretation of tongues—all of us are given gifts for ministry and service, and so no one member of the body is valued more than another.

At the same time, however, the church has always needed some way to order itself. We know from the book of Acts that deacons were chosen early in the church's life. The letters to Timothy, probably written near the end of the first century, mention bishops, who may well have been presbyters, or ministers, of a congregation (see 1 Tim. 3). There is evidence that by the middle of the second century, worshiping communities had appointed presiders (or presidents), people designated to preach and give thanks over the bread and cup in the context of the many ministries of the assembly. Some would offer prayers, some present the gifts of bread and wine. Some would read the sacred texts, some would serve the Lord's Supper, others would take up the collection. Worship, then, would be led by various members of the body, with one of their number called out to preach and pray over the bread and the cup. From early on, then, the church recognized the need for someone who would make sure the church did what it was created to do—to tell the story and celebrate the mysteries of God, so that the whole body of Christ could go and act them out in the world.

Calvin, too, thought that there was "a need for a voice within the community that proclaimed God's word and presided at the sacraments."[5] It was not enough for Christians to puzzle over Scripture alone, outside of a community of believers; they needed to gather to hear, understand, and apply the Word to their lives. So God gathers the church and calls forth some to be such a voice within the community of faith. In other words, sooner or later someone must rise from the assembly to speak. Someone must be chosen—be called out—to proclaim the good news in speech and in sign. It is not only a matter of order, however; we need someone who has come from our midst to take on the profound burden of speaking God's blessing to us. We need one who will, in the words of Catherine Gunsalus González, "proclaim in speech and sacrament the word of God to the people of God."[6] Or, as William Seth Adams has put it, we need someone to be "the community's sayer of grace."[7] Those who are chosen for the task are called from the community of the baptized, and this is the foundation upon which any discussion of what it means to be a leader of worship—to preside—must be built.

Presiding in worship, then, involves an inherent tension. On the one hand, we nurture the deep conviction that the church is a priesthood of all believers.

In our baptism we are made one, and each member of the body is considered equal to all others. On the other hand, we recognize that the community needs members who are set apart for particular tasks. To be called out and set apart is to be endowed with a certain authority. This is not authority *over* the people, however, but authority *for* the people, authority that rests only on the Word of God and not on any notion of ecclesiastical hierarchy—and certainly not on any fiction that one who is called out is (or has any hope of ever being) holier than any other of the baptized. Scott Haldeman has put it well:

> There is one ministry of the church that extends from the font to the promised "river of life." Born in the womb of baptism, the church and all its members walk steadily on toward the new Jerusalem, where God will dwell with God's people, where there will be no more death and every tear will be wiped away. The ordained are not the only ones on this journey— all the baptized must go the distance. As we have seen, the ministry of all is communal, demanding and daunting; yet the font provides sufficient strength. . . . All of us are to speak good news to our neighbors. All of us are to participate in and nurture the Body. All of us are to participate in public prayer. All of us are to preserve the truth and promote justice. All of us are to point out signs of God's promised future. These are not things that only pastors, deacons and elders do. Washed, all of us are made ready to serve.
>
> We need leaders, certainly. . . . We need those who call us back to the waters, and to the bread and to the wine, so that weary arms are revived and stale visions are replaced by fresh imaginings of what could be, what has been promised, and where we must go next. The Body requires such service. . . . But those called out from among the Body are not to function as the Body, only to help the Body function.[8]

Servant of the Assembly

How then should we imagine the one who presides? Ask a room full of people who have spent any time at all in one form or another of Christian worship, and the answers will be surprisingly similar. Ask, "What qualities do you appreciate in a worship leader?" and you will hear things like presence, authenticity, warmth, grace, humor, reverence. Ask what characteristics you hope you never see again, and the list is usually even longer: lack of energy, easily distracted, no eye contact, distant, dull, verbose. As with good art or great music, we may not be able to explain what makes a good worship leader, but we often know it when we see it—and when we don't.

So what model is there for one who is called out from the midst of the body to be a leader of worship? Any number of images have been suggested.

Kierkegaard's scheme of worship as theater is well known: the members of the congregation are the chief actors, God is the audience, and the pastor serves as prompter for the actors, who are the primary worshipers. William Seth Adams has put forth the idea of a conductor of an orchestra. The conductor's work depends on the musicians assembled and on their willingness to follow his or her lead, which means that a certain reciprocity is required.[9] Elaine Ramshaw has suggested that the pastor who leads worship is like a midwife for the people's labor. "She presides, leads, directs, and organizes, all to help the people of God do *their* work: the lectors' reading, the assistant ministers' speaking or chanting, the whole assembly's movement and singing and phrasing of petitions in prayer, . . . a good presider is one who draws her congregation into the ancient dance with a new song."[10] Other images have occurred to people along the way—father or mother figure, resident theologian, enabler, and (though few would own up to it) talk-show host, or emcee of a variety show.

The best models convey that it is the gathered assembly that is the chief actor, the central symbol, in Christian worship. This assembly is not just a collection of individuals (or consumers) who are serviced, but also a gathering of people among whom has been cultivated a sense of community and an awareness that they have assembled for their shared work of worship.[11] The presider may be best understood, then, as the *servant of the assembly*, the one who, as Gordon Lathrop has expressed it, "by word and by bearing, with dignity and focus and love, invite[s] a community to gather around the central signs" of book, bath, and meal.[12]

This means that while the assembly is the chief symbol in worship, the presider, or pastor, also has symbolic weight. As Lathrop has pointed out, "We need such a symbol among us, and we would be fooling ourselves if we thought we could live without it. A responsible steward of the mysteries awakens among us the hope for Mystery."[13] Yet this symbol is one that must, in Lathrop's parlance, be "broken," since those who lead in worship live within this tension of being one called out from the body, that is, as one who presides in the midst of the priesthood of all believers.[14] "Trustworthy pastors," he says, "will always realize with both humility and relief" that they are not the shepherds of the flock, but that they point

> beyond themselves to the One who lives at the heart of the assembly's symbols. Trustworthy pastors will be transparent to the one Shepherd. And trustworthy pastors will know that the Spirit of God raises up many people in the assembly with the gift of leading others to pasture and freedom. Taking up the challenges and tasks of this paradoxical title, the inversions of this broken symbol, can rightly fill up a lifetime of good work.[15]

This is not an easy thing, to live in the tension between recognizing, on the one hand, the symbolic weight and significance of being one who presides in worship, and on the other, the need for humility and transparency. We can indeed live there, though, if we understand ourselves as servants of the assembly and stewards of the kingdom of God.

Enacting the Reign of God

In the final scene of the film *Places in the Heart*, a remarkable thing takes place. We see worshipers gathered in a small country church. The church is in Waxahachie, Texas, and the year is 1935. There aren't many people there, but the faithful few who are scattered around the little sanctuary stand and sing "Blessed Assurance" with as much fervor as they can muster. The minister reads from Scripture, familiar words about love from the thirteenth chapter of First Corinthians. As he reads, the wife of a man who has been discovered in an adulterous affair takes his hand for the first time since she learned of his terrible secret. This is no syrupy hand-holding to sweet-sounding words of love, but the gesture of a woman determined to live out the gospel she believes no matter how painful, a gesture received by a man who knows that forgiveness and reconciliation come at a price.

Soon it is time for Communion, and the tiny choir stands to sing "I Come to the Garden Alone." While they sing, we watch the worshipers pass plates of bread cubes and small glasses of grape juice down the pews. It gradually becomes clear that there are more people in those pews than when the service began. Sharing the body and blood of Christ are all the people we have seen throughout the film: the bank president who tried to foreclose on a young widow; the white men who lynched a black boy after he mistakenly shot the town's beloved sheriff; the players in the honky-tonk band and the floozies who followed them from dance to dance; Moze, the African American laborer who had helped the young widow bring a prizewinning crop of cotton to save her farm, and the Klansmen who drove him out of town; and, finally, the sheriff himself and the boy who had killed him. "The peace of Christ," the sheriff says to the boy as he shares the bread and wine. "The peace of Christ," the boy whispers in return. Here, at the Lord's Table, life triumphs over death, love overcomes hatred, mercy covers guilt, and those who could not or would not live together in peace are reconciled in Christ's name. It is not reality, but a vision—yet it is a vision more real than any earthly truth. It is a vision of the coming reign of God.

This is the vision we enact whenever we gather for worship. We are made equal, and equally beloved, in baptism. We proclaim that gospel when we read and preach Scripture. We gather at the table where all are welcome, and there is plenty for all. "Liturgy is a kingdom scene," says Robert Hovda,

> where people are supposed to be naked, stripped of their daily burdens and statuses (even of their sex and color) and the only thing that can make tolerable such a surrender of our defences is a palpable corporate consciousness of God. Before God, we are sisters and brothers only, and if we cannot find, or lose, the sense of mystery and reverence we are thrown back on our clothes or class or work, back into a relatively trivial situation which cannot support common prayer.[16]

In other words, we enact a vision in worship where all are equal in the sight of God, and all are treated as such, with dignity and love. We act out the grace that all receive, poured out in equal and abundant measure. We live out, in our worship—and at our most faithful, in the world—that vision where the rules of the world cease to have any power and God's realm is the one that is really real. In enacting together the promised reign of God, we lean expectantly into the coming of the kingdom even as we wait and pray for it. It is an *active* waiting, where we describe the vision with our words and act it out with our hands and feet and faces—indeed, with our whole bodies.

This is work that changes us. As Lathrop puts it, "we are made a holy people," something new, something we would not otherwise be.[17] Adams puts it another way, explaining that the worshiping community "is the showingforth of the Body of Christ in tangible human form. There members of the Body are reconstituted by the liturgy into what can never be shown forth so fully or with such power in any other time or manner."[18] To be sure, this is the work of the whole community, and the presider is the steward of that work.

Hungering for Epiphany

It is gradually becoming clear that leading in worship requires more than a particular combination of skills, techniques, and charisma. There is deep spiritual work involved here, and the best presiders do not shy away from it. This is not easy to do, because it means being open to mystery and relinquishing our fear of losing control. It is essential, however, for worshipers to come "hungering for an epiphany," as one pastor has put it, and those who are called out to be liturgical leaders dare not sell them short.[19]

The temptation to do otherwise is constant. Instead of coming to worship expecting to meet God, creating space for divine encounter, we limit the possibilities by filling every moment with chatter and business. Edward Farley calls our bluff:

> To attend the typical Protestant Sunday morning worship service is to experience something odd, something like a charade. The discourse (invocation, praises, hymns, confessions, sacred texts) indicates that the event celebrates a sacred presence. But this discourse is neutralized by the prevailing mood, which is casual, comfortable, chatty, busy, humorous, pleasant and at times even cute. This mood is a sign not of a sacred reality but of various congregational self-preoccupations.[20]

Farley is on to something, and regardless of our tradition or style of worship we need to heed his words. We pray in such a passionless tone that no one could be expected to enter into prayer. We put more energy into the announcements than we do into our Communion liturgies, and insist on explaining everything to death. We parade newly baptized babies around, coaxing the cooing of the congregation as though this child had not just been saved from death and delivered from the worst the world can do. Or we rush through the words, saying them by rote, using as little water as possible so we can hurry through a neat and well-packaged ceremony in order to get on with the rest of the service. We nibble on a pinch of bread and wash it down with a thimbleful of grape juice, forgetting our own deep hunger, the hunger of our communities and of the world, settling instead for a private moment with Jesus. Or we dispense with the sacrament altogether, figuring that it is really not so important to modern people such as ourselves. We have stopped expecting God to show up in worship.

Some of us experience other temptations. Sometimes those who are the most gifted for the work of leading the body in the worship of God are so gifted, in fact, that they become the "stars" of the liturgy. We enjoy the laughter we evoke when we are entertaining in our preaching or presiding. We love being the one up front, and we know we are good at it. Yet even our best gifts can get in the way of making space to encounter the holy. As Hovda puts it, if the presider "fails to communicate a sense of prayerful performance, of *being (first of all) a worshiper and a member of the worshiping assembly*, then he or she is not a leader but an intruder. And the gifts of such a one or such a group damage rather than enhance worship."[21] Even our own talent can get in the way of seeking an encounter with the holy.

And so we all need to come hungering for an epiphany. Yes, as worship leaders we bring our best to our work, but not for the sake of being wonderful presiders. Rather, as Hovda says, we bring "a God-consciousness so awesome, so strong, so powerful that all participants are focused not on ourselves and our many splendid gifts, but on our common and mysterious Source, on the only One who is Holy."[22]

It is important, of course, to acknowledge that every congregation is different and that all worship is contextual. Those who would plan and lead worship must consider the particularities of the community that gathers. In some churches, a great deal of attention is given to the forming of community, and this is apparent in their church's worship life. Other congregations place more emphasis on seeking an experience of the transcendent in worship. This is not to say that churches should do one or the other—ideally, all congregations will intentionally build community and also crave transcendence! Yet most congregations fall at various points along the scale. Decisions about worship will also be made based, in part, on whether congregations are large or small; rural, urban, or suburban; poor, wealthy, or somewhere in the middle. In every situation, however, the church gathers to worship God, and the worship of the Holy One is what must remain central to our decisions about what happens in worship and how.

In every context, then, we must make space for the holy. In some places that might mean entering into fervent prayer, whether extemporaneous or written, or urging worshipers on to a more lively expression. In other places it might mean cultivating silence. In any case, in order to make space for the holy—or perhaps to get out of the way of divine encounter so as not to prevent it—those who lead worship must also come hungering for an epiphany, expecting to be changed, and communicating that expectancy and openness to those who gather for worship. For we come to be shaped and formed by something—Someone—greater than ourselves and to be part of something more than ourselves. Those of us who lead worship must learn the techniques, do the preparatory work, and hone our skills—and then we must let go of our cravings for affection, admiration, and affirmation, and give up our perfectionist anxieties. It's something like working without a net—you train and practice, you come prepared to be part of a remarkable holy drama, but in the end you give yourself over to the Holy One.

Nothing in worship is pro forma, then; even when we are speaking familiar words and enacting well-worn rituals, it is with the awareness that we are on holy ground. Hovda says, "Presiding in liturgy, because it is the common deed of the entire church, requires a kind of modest prayerfulness that is heavy on awe and mystery, light on answers and recipes."[23] Those are good words to guide us into this exploration of what it means to preside in worship in the midst of God's people, dedicating body, mind, and spirit to the task.

The Worshiping Body

Most of us understand that preparing for worship involves intellectual engagement, and the best of us recognize that there is a spiritual component at work as well. Many of us, however, have a harder time imagining ourselves as bringing our *bodies* to the task of leading worship. Except for the dancers—and perhaps the athletes—among us, many presiders, at least in the "mainline" traditions, present themselves as people with capable minds and faithful spirits who are utterly detached from the torsos and arms and feet that reside somewhere below their necks.

Worshiping, however, is a fully embodied act, and so presiders necessarily lead worship as embodied people. In other words, we bring our minds, spirits, *and* bodies to the work of presiding. It's not just a matter of performing better. As anthropologist Talal Asad speculates, "the inability to 'enter into communion with God' becomes a function of untaught bodies." Furthermore, he asserts that the more experienced the human body, "the less its dependence on language."[24] Now, as people of the Book, we are not about to give up our words, nor should we. But if we realize that we bring not only our minds and spirits, and our words, but also our *bodies* to worship—that is, if we cultivate our physical engagement along with our intellectual and spiritual engagement—we open up a greater space for meeting God.

This book begins where most of us are most comfortable—with our minds and, to some extent, with our spirits. Now that we have established a framework for understanding who a presider is, and what a presider does, we will turn to the body of the presider, and how it informs the work that we do. Chapter 2 will lay the foundation for understanding the embodied nature of worship by exploring biblical precedents and examining the liturgical and ethical implications. Chapter 3, on eyes and ears, is devoted to preparing for worship by attending to the world around us, the life among us, and the work of the Spirit within us. In chapter 4, on the mouth, the focus is on the power of the voice and the nature of liturgical speech. Chapters 5 and 6, on hands and feet, move from the realm of speech to explore gesture, touch, and movement in worship. We will consider the power of the hands to communicate and to bless, then explore how the feet move the whole body, enabling presiders to use movement and space. In chapter 7 the conversation moves to the heart, delving more deeply into the spirituality of presiding and what it means to preside with love, passion, and humility.

The more worship leaders give thought to the weighty responsibility of leading people in worship, the more we know, in our heart of hearts, that this task requires all we have to give—and sometimes more than we think we have. As we embark on this journey into what it means to preside in worship, we remember what is proclaimed in the Presbyterian commissioning service: whatever it is you are summoned to do, your baptism is sufficient for your calling.

For Further Reading

William Seth Adams. *Shaped by Images: One Who Presides.* New York: Church Publishing, 1995.

Robert W. Hovda. *Strong, Loving, and Wise: Presiding in Liturgy.* 5th ed. Collegeville, MN: Liturgical Press, 1981.

Chapter 2

The Embodied Nature of Worship

The Body of Christ

To consider worship as an embodied event is to explore all the various ways bodies are involved in meeting God. We are the body of Christ; we are fed by Christ's body; we encounter the divine in bodily experience; we worship with our bodies; we tend to others' bodies as part of our Christian vocation. In short, to acknowledge the embodied nature of worship—indeed, of Christian discipleship—is to explore the sacramentality of all of life. This is familiar territory for Catholic and Orthodox traditions, but less so for many Protestant traditions. Yet even Calvin recognized the sacramental nature of the created order. The tree of life was a sign of immortality for Adam and Eve, he says. The rainbow God hung for Noah to see was a sign of God's promise to never destroy the earth again. The tree and the rainbow were considered sacraments by Adam and Eve and Noah. "When they were inscribed by God's word a new form was put upon them, so that they began to be what previously they were not." Even now, he argues, we see the rainbow as a sign of God's promise. "If God had imprinted such reminders on the sun, stars, earth, stones, they would all be sacraments for us."[1] For Calvin there is a distinction, of course, between sacramental signs and the "ordinary sacraments of the church," but there is, nevertheless, a recognition that God speaks to humans through material things. God takes the common elements of our lives and uses them so that we might apprehend something of who God is.

The same thing is true in worship. Something remarkable happens when Christians gather for worship; God takes us as we are and does a new thing. Just as Jesus took common elements of bread and wine and made them holy things, so God makes us a holy people, something we would not be otherwise.[2] When we come together as the worshiping body, we are not just a col-

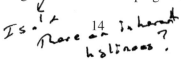

Is. Peace on Inherit
14 holiness?

lection of individuals who happen to be in the same place at the same time. To put it in the words of William Seth Adams, we are "the showing forth of the Body of Christ in tangible human form."[3]

The body of Christ. We can thank Paul for this language, of course. Writing to that contentious little group of believers in Corinth, he told them they could not do without each other. "The body does not consist of one member but of many," he wrote. "If the foot would say, 'Because I am not a hand, I do not belong to the body,' that would not make it any less a part of the body. And if the ear would say, 'Because I am not an eye, I do not belong to the body,' that would not make it any less a part of the body. . . . There are many members, yet one body" (1 Cor. 12:14–16, 20).

In fact, Paul goes on, "the members of the body that seem to be weaker are indispensable, and those members of the body that we think less honorable we clothe with greater honor." The church is like that, he says: "God has so arranged the body, giving the greater honor to the inferior member, that there may be no dissension within the body, but the members may have the same care for one another. If one member suffers, all suffer together with it; if one member is honored, all rejoice together with it" (1 Cor. 12:22–23, 24–26).

This is familiar language for Christians, but it was proclaimed to me with new power soon after I began teaching at Columbia Theological Seminary. A group from the Metro State Women's Prison visited the campus, not to talk about the realities of incarceration, but to lead us in worship. They had traded their prison khakis for white choir robes and sang as the Voices of Hope choir. White and black, young and not-so-young, they sang about Jesus and being saved and having hope. They made us cry and they cried too. Then one of them, a young African American woman, preached.

"It is God who chooses us," she said, "God who places us in a unique position within the body of Christ. He chooses one eye with 20/20 vision and places it beside an eye that is half blind. Then he selects an aching hand and attaches it to a powerful arm. He finds a sprained ankle and he strengthens it so it can lift up a leg that was once fractured. Then he searches and searches until he finds a powerful chest and teaches it by example to embrace a broken heart. Then God binds together each part with love and he sends his Holy Spirit coursing through its veins until it is moved and motivated to stand up and step out—step out into the community, into prisons, into the wilderness, to prepare the way for the Word of God." Then she looked at us. "Look within you. Look around you. This is the body of Christ," she proclaimed, sweeping her arm over us all—all of us in the pews, and all the women in the choir. "We are the body of Christ."[4]

She described us to a T, each of us a little battered, all of us a little broken, no one of us completely strong or self-sufficient, but in need of the others. Those of us who would not return to locked cells at night knew that we were attached to those sisters, and that the body was not complete without them. We knew it because we were there, worshiping together—not because we read about it in an essay, or because an esteemed member of the faculty told us so. What we knew in our minds already, we now knew in our souls—in our bodies—because we were worshiping there, together, in the flesh.

In the first chapter of this book we acknowledged that when Christians come together, we gather to *do* something. When we are initiated into the body of Christ, it is accomplished not only through what we say, but also through what we do. We head for the water, whether it is a river or a baptistry or a font, so that it can be poured over our bodies. After the washing, we gather around the Lord's Table that we might be fed and therefore sustained as the body of Christ. In other words, God makes us church through the things we do with our bodies: speaking and hearing the Word, baptizing, and sharing the meal Christ gives us. Theologian Louis-Marie Chauvet would persuade us that in these acts God chooses our embodied selves as the place of revelation. "The sacraments state that the word of God wants to enter our bodies, that is, our lives," he asserts, "and that for anyone in-dwelt by the Spirit the road of the God of Jesus Christ necessarily uses the human road."[5] Indeed, this has been true since the beginning of the Christian story, when one young woman was chosen to become the mother of Jesus, the God-bearer, Theotokos. Those who would pray in Advent with the Church of Scotland would affirm this remarkable way God deals with humans:

> God and maker of all,
> to redeem the world
> you chose the most unsuspecting of women
> to mother your Son
> and by your choice gave new glory
> to human flesh and earthly parenting.
>
> With the joy that was Mary's,
> may our souls magnify the Lord,
> and our bodies be the means
> through which you continue
> the mighty work of salvation
> for which Christ came.
> Amen.[6]

The Embodied Nature of Worship

Although we may understand ourselves metaphorically as the body of Christ, and embrace the incarnation of Jesus as essential to Christian belief, many of us do not readily recognize the bodily nature of Christian worship. We live in an era when folks bemoan the shrinking of the church and try virtually any method that promises to attract more people, especially younger ones. Many of these younger folks already know what the rest of us have forgotten—that vital and faithful worship involves the whole person—mind, spirit, and *body*. Drawing on the work of anthropologists, theologian Sarah Coakley asserts that "religious beliefs are embodied through religious practices. In fact, the practices may be said to precede the belief."[7] In other words, body and mind work in concert to nurture faith. Belief is more than doctrinal affirmations; it is something we act out as much as it is something we profess. Or, to put it another way, believing involves our whole selves—our thinking selves as well as our physical selves. Samuel Torvend goes so far as to say that "the great qualities of life, what Christians call the gifts of God—love, mercy, grace, hope—are always, always *mediated bodily* through word and gesture, word and sign, human voice and earthy sacrament."[8]

Bringing our whole selves to worship means recognizing that *we not only have bodies, we are bodies.* Consider the well-known story of the road to Emmaus (Luke 24:13–35). Cleopas and another disciple are making their way down the road when they encounter a stranger. They tell him all about the prophet Jesus, who was killed, and how, after three days, some women of their group had found him missing from his tomb. Angels had told the women that Jesus was alive, but these disciples have no proof, and they are trying desperately to make sense of it all. As they walk, the stranger talks to them about Moses and the prophets and how this Messiah's death was necessary. Dusk falls, and they stop for dinner, and when the stranger breaks bread before them, "their eyes were opened, and they recognized him." And then they remember: "Were not our hearts burning within us while he was talking to us on the road, while he was opening the scriptures to us?" These two disciples did not simply have an intellectual insight. They realized Jesus' identity in their very bodies—their eyes were opened; their hearts burned. They experienced Christ and learned firsthand that *the body is the locus of the experience of the holy.*

There is a little spot on the Eastern Shore of Maryland that is the most beautiful place I know. When I am there, my whole body changes. I breathe in the slightly salty, slightly marshy air, taking in as much as I possibly can. I feel my spirits lift as I encounter so much beauty and wildness. I feel elation somewhere in my midsection—that feeling of awe and gratitude that is like nothing else—and an expansiveness that convinces me, all over again, that God is alive and loose in the world. The feelings evoked by this place are physical ones—they are more than pleasant ideas.

It works the same way with feelings of grief: our chests fill until it seems they might burst; our bodies ache when we are grieving. So it is with experiences of God. It may feel like a sense of overwhelming peace or an electrical shock. It may result in tears or trembling, or a deep calm. A "spiritual experience" is physical indeed—we feel an encounter with the divine in our bodies. It is important to acknowledge that feeling is not the only indicator of God's presence; God is present even when we do not feel a thing. Yet our experiences of God happen to our embodied selves.

Just as personal experiences of God happen in our individual bodies, we meet the divine communally in our collective body. It is *together* that we constitute the body of Christ, and God is mediated to us through our encounters with one another. Chauvet insists that "the gospel is communitarian by its very nature. To believe in Christ is to be immediately gathered together by him who is confessed as 'our' common Lord." He continues, "Christians are people who join their sisters and brothers in an assembly in the name and memory of Jesus. Such an assembly is the Christians' *primary mark . . .* the 'fundamental sacrament' of the risen Christ."[9] Even the most common details of our life together can show forth Christ to us. One Sunday after I had communed I watched as others in the congregation received bread and wine. After one of our pastors had taken the bread and wine, she passed by me, licking her fingers, and I could see just how good is the goodness of God. Not every showing forth is so winsome, though, and living together as a body does not happen naturally. We are flawed and fragile human beings who don't always like each other very much. We are *made* the body of Christ by the work of the Spirit.

In a compelling memoir of her conversion to faith called *Take This Bread,* Sara Miles tells the story of how she was called by God—one might even say *driven* by God—to begin a food pantry in her church, St. Gregory of Nyssa Episcopal Church in San Francisco. It wasn't an easy idea to sell to the congregation. They were a faith community made up of artists and scholars, a mostly upper-middle-class group of folks who cared a great deal about the beauty of their building and the impact this ministry would have on their polite neighborhood. They were worried about how they would find enough money, or get enough volunteers, and how they could sustain such an ambitious venture. After no small amount of arguing, though, they agreed, more or less, to go through with it, and on the first day about thirty people came for food. Soon they were giving groceries to nearly three hundred people each week.

Every Friday, a truck from the San Francisco Food Bank would pull up to the church doors and deliver pallets full of cereal and bread and fresh fruits and vegetables that would be given, free, to those who didn't have enough food to go around. Sara and others from the church would bring the food right into the sanctuary and display it around the Communion table, the place of feeding, and folks from the community would come and choose what they needed to cook good meals for their families.

One day the driver from the Food Bank paused to look at the unique baptismal font at the church. It stood just outside the side door of the sanctuary—large, rough-hewn rocks with water cascading down them into a pool. "That's where I was baptized," Sara said. The driver was silent for a moment. An evangelical Christian, he probably would have been scandalized by the liberal politics and theology at St. Gregory's. He knew that Sara was a lesbian. She knew he kept a King James Bible in the cab of his truck, because all other versions were heretical.

After a while, still looking at the baptistry, the driver finally spoke. "And the thing is," he said, "he brought water, *water,* out of the rock."

"Yes," said Sara, "and that rock is Christ."

For all their differences, they were connected by a story, by a biblical tradition—an unlikely pair joined by their common baptism, made one with Christ and also with one another. They were further bound by their common calling, "the rough wooden pallet of onions that organized [their] days"—that is, their calling to feed people.[10]

When we come together for worship, then, we constitute the body of Christ in a multilayered way. We carry in our bodies our particularities—our memories and experiences, the places we have lived and the things that have happened to us—and yet at the same time we are bound by the gospel we share and formed by our communal worship. The water that washes us, the stories we tell, and the bread and wine that feed us, all make us who we are and shape our way of living in the world. Theologian Bruce Morrill puts it this way:

> The assembled person-bodies together constitute the unique members of the body of Christ, the Church. The ritual body, in word and sacrament, obtains a knowledge of the Church and the world in relationship to God, but always within a body of culture, a social context wherein the story of salvation is mysteriously coming about. The Church takes confidence in a multiplicity of bodies and histories as the very "place" of humanity's redemption on the basis of the Gospel, wherein the Holy Spirit creates,

guides, and raises up the body of Jesus as Christ, animates the Church as Christ's body for the life of the world, and sustains believers with the eucharistic body of the Lord at the center of all the ritual sacraments.[11]

In other words, the Holy Spirit creates a new oneness out of all our varied bodies and histories, thereby constituting the body of Christ from our "assembled person-bodies" who gather to do something in worship. We are baptized into this body. We are sustained, comforted, and fueled by the very body of Christ, the eucharistic body. Our particularities are not erased, but the Spirit gives the means and power to make us one, that we might be sent into the world to be a new creation, Christ's own body, there.

We know, of course, that the path is not always smooth, and that professing our oneness as the body of Christ does not mean we always know how to live out that unity. Although the church constitutes a body with shared rituals, different parts of the body of Christ construe those shared rituals in different ways. Whether we are Anglican or Pentecostal, we gather having agreed on particular patterns of behavior. Those patterns may include kneeling and chanting or jumping and speaking in tongues. Quakers agree to wait in silence until the Spirit moves someone to speak. In my mother's youth, folks in worship would "get happy" and hop across the backs of the pews. Many (but not all) African American churches have agreed-upon patterns of singing, clapping, or urging on the preacher. To be sure, these various patterns can look quite different from one another, and some members of the body may be suspicious of the practices of others, keeping us separate from one another. But sometimes our commonality as embodied people of faith enables us to overcome our differences in surprising and redeeming ways.

Morrill tells the story of an African American woman named Betty who had left behind her Baptist upbringing and converted to Catholicism, something her family never understood. When Betty died, her own parish priest was away, and Father Morrill, who was associated with a nearby parish, was asked to preside at the funeral. His contact at Betty's church, Sister Alice, explained to him that Betty had been estranged from her kin ever since she became a Catholic, and the family was not expected to show up for the funeral. Nevertheless, the church wanted there to be a respectable showing at the service, and since Betty had not been a member for long, Sister Alice was gathering about a dozen folks from the congregation to be present.

When Father Morrill arrived at Betty's church, he was surprised to find about a hundred people lined up and waiting, all members of Betty's family. He and Sister Alice quickly put their heads together, and decided they would celebrate the Roman Catholic liturgy with this Baptist congregation, explaining the elements of the service along the way.

They soon found out that the family members were not lined up for the procession that was part of the Roman Catholic liturgy, but rather to see the body before the service, which is the practice of believers in their Baptist tradition. Father Morrill explained that according to Roman Catholic practice, everyone would take part in a procession into the sanctuary. He told them that the white cloth covering the coffin was to represent a baptismal garment, and they sprinkled water over it to remember Betty's baptism. Then they all processed into the church together, behind the crucifix and the coffin, symbolizing the way Betty first entered the church. When it came time for the homily, Father Morrill preached on Romans 6, which is all about dying and rising with Christ in baptism. Baptism was their connection, the source of their common identity—but it was also a part of what made them different.

Father Morrill then talked about the Eucharist that would follow—how the gifts of bread and wine would be brought forward by members of the community, the body of Christ—how the bread and wine were symbols of the people's own labor, and about to become the eucharistic body and blood of Christ. At the time of the Eucharist, he knew his polity would not allow him to share that bread and wine with the visiting Baptists, and so he invited those who wanted it to receive a blessing. As he walked among the people, he first encountered Betty's sister. Yes, she wanted a blessing. So he traced the sign of the cross on her head—and she raised her hands in prayer, and stood that way, swaying. There they were, the priest with his hand on her head, she with her arms outstretched in prayer, and they stood that way for a long time. And so it went, with person after person, as they stood together—hand on head, arms outstretched, swaying, sometimes singing, sometimes praying.

Writing about the experience later, Morrill said, "Baptist sisters and brothers were entering into communion in a way consonant with their own tradition of ritual prayer. Communion was taking place for and among us in a way I had never experienced, and it was an embodied, incorporated and corporeal, form of communion, indeed."[12] For all of the hospitality shown, the explanations given, the words spoken, it was those unspoken, physical expressions that allowed them to enter into communion with Christ and with one another, creating space for an encounter with the holy and bridging the chasms that separated people of different traditions.

The body is a powerful conduit for expression and experience; what we do with our bodies has the capacity to bear meaning beyond what our words can articulate. But it doesn't always come easy. The poet Jane Kenyon has written about "the long struggle to be at home in the body, this difficult friendship."[13]

Indeed, it has been our struggle since creation. God created the world and called it good, blessing the bodies formed by divine hands. And yet, according to classical understandings of the fall, our bodies were (and are) the places of brokenness, vulnerable to sin and apt to harm the bodies of others. In the Christian story, redemption comes through the body of God made flesh, and this time brokenness brings forth wholeness and the healing of all the nations. The "long struggle" is embedded in the narrative of God's history with God's people.

This "difficult friendship" is furthermore played out in our own lives. North Americans live in a time and place where the body has become idealized and sexualized; the images of the body that bombard us daily present perfectly toned, coiffed, and made-up airbrushed figures that have more to do with fantasy than reality. For some of us, our bodies become our enemies as we try to make them thinner or younger or more attractive. Falling far short of those ubiquitous images of perfection, it seems that few of us revel in our bodies as magnificent gifts of a creative, creating God. Yet the revitalization of worship in many parts of the church depends, in part, on our reclaiming our bodiliness and rediscovering the embodied nature of our worship.

This is really not such a new idea; in fact, if we explore the symbols and rituals of the church's traditions, we find that embedded in the rich history of worship are myriad ways that God leads us into an encounter with the divine. Light, color, sound, gesture, touch—we apprehend all of these with our bodies, and God uses them all in order to meet us. Think, for example, of how light affects worship—praying in the full morning sun is a different experience than praying in the evening shadows, by candlelight. For some, color is a powerful communicator as well, evoking the mood or tone of a day or season. Or think of how sounds draw forth varying responses from us: the unmitigated triumph of Easter morning trumpets prompt our full-throated songs of joy and praise, while the sound of a single, plaintive oboe invites us into a song of lament.

I once served as liturgist at a summer worship and music conference, where the week's lectionary included some challenging texts. In one service, the Scripture readings of the day included a text of judgment in which the prophet warned the people of what God would do to an unfaithful Israel. As it turned out, the person who had signed up to read Scripture that day was a child. I wondered whether we should try to make some sort of change, perhaps arranging for her to read on another day when the text would not sound so ominous. But time was short, and it was decided that we would go on as planned. The little girl proclaimed the prophet's words, and we were amazed. In the voice of a booming baritone, we would have heard only the threat of the wrath of God. In the voice of a little girl, we heard the same words, yet were aware of how, at the root of it all, our trust is in the God who is in covenant with us, that God's judgment is the way God corrects us, guides us, and refines us. All because of the sound of a voice and the sight of the small person from which that voice emerged.

Worshipers often experience the embodied nature of worship through singing together. I once took part in a church's 150th anniversary celebration that included a hymn festival. The expert musicians who had come for the event dazzled us with their creativity and skill. We sang inventive arrangements and gloried in brilliant improvisations. The most remarkable thing of all, though, was watching as people sang an old familiar hymn, "Great Is Thy Faithfulness." They sang their hearts out—some with their eyes closed and faces upturned, some with tears streaming down their cheeks, all bound together by the sound of their joined voices and the feeling of vibration in the room that came from all that singing and their shared trust in a faithful God.

These are but a few examples of what we already know. God is more than an idea to be contemplated; God is made present in our midst, mediated to us through our very bodies, through taste and touch, sight and sound. The transcendent God who is so far beyond our comprehension is also God incarnate, the Word who is made flesh and speaks that Word to, and through, our own beautifully imperfect frames, surprising us with divine graces and binding us to one another in ways that would be otherwise impossible.

The Body and the Bible

Near the end of Mark's Gospel is an astonishing scene. Jesus is in Bethany at the house of a friend. They are sitting at table when a woman comes in, unannounced. She carries with her an alabaster jar, a beautiful thing indeed. Without saying a word she breaks open the jar, releasing the exquisite scent of the rare and expensive perfume inside. She pours the precious ointment over the head of Jesus—no carefully rationed dab of this treasured substance, no small drip, but an outpouring of all there is. She is chided for her wastefulness by some, but Jesus defends her. "She has performed a good service for me," he says. "She has done what she could; she has anointed my body beforehand for its burial" (Mark 14:6b, 8). In one simple but extravagant act, this unnamed woman says more than she might have with words: this One, this Holy One, is to be adored; we do homage to his divinity by attending with love and care to his very body. And Jesus, for his part, approves. "Wherever the good news is proclaimed in the whole world," he declares, "what she has done will be told in remembrance of her" (14:9). This unnamed woman's deed proclaims to us that Jesus is no disembodied holy being; he is an embodied human being, and a faithful one's attention to his body was a very good thing. This is but one example of how the body is esteemed in Scripture; if we peruse the Bible from Genesis to Revelation, we find a high view of the human body expressed throughout. Even a brief survey of texts shows that, for biblical writers, the body matters.

It all begins, of course, with Genesis. In the first account of creation, God makes humankind, male and female, in the divine image, and blesses them (Gen. 1:27–28). In the second narrative, God creates the earth and the heavens, then makes a person out of the dust of the ground, forming a human being from the very earth. God breathes life into this being; the human's breath is God's own (Gen. 2:4b–8). Having been made of earth's own matter, we humans are connected to creation, and yet we are *only* dust, mortal—at once sacred and vulnerable.

If the Genesis accounts tell us about the creating of the first humans, the psalmist sings about the making of us all. We were imagined by God even before we were formed, the psalmist says, knit together by that same divine Creator (Ps. 139:13–16). We are remarkable creatures, "fearfully and wonderfully made," connected to the expansiveness of the cosmos, yet, at the same time, intimately known. This God not only knows our innermost thoughts, but has also shaped our bodies into glorious beings.

It is hard to imagine any more expressive adoration of this glorious human body than that of the Song of Songs, that set of luscious love poems in which the lovers extol one another's beauty. "The voice of my beloved!" the female lover cries out.

> Look, he comes,
> leaping upon the mountains,
>   bounding over the hills.
> My beloved is like a gazelle
>   or a young stag.
>   (Song 2:8–9a)

The male lover is even more loquacious when he adores his bride:

> How graceful are your feet in sandals,
>   O queenly maiden!
> Your rounded thighs are like jewels,
>   the work of a master hand.
> Your navel is a rounded bowl
>   that never lacks mixed wine.

> Your belly is a heap of wheat,
>   encircled with lilies.
> Your two breasts are like two fawns,
>   twins of a gazelle.
> Your neck is like an ivory tower.
> Your eyes are pools in Heshbon,
>   by the gate of Bath-rabbim.
> Your nose is like a tower of Lebanon,
>   overlooking Damascus.
> Your head crowns you like Carmel,
>   and your flowing locks are like purple;
>   a king is held captive in the tresses.
>   (Song 7:1–5)

There is more, of course, much more, but even these few verses are enough to recall the utter gloriousness of the human body. These bodies God made are beautiful, even stunning, and worthy of adoration.

Because these bodies are so precious, so remarkable, so glorious, they are to be honored. As glorious as the human body is, it is not made solely for pleasure, but also for service, nurture, worship, and birthing. It is clear throughout the Hebrew biblical tradition that the body is to be honored in the context of covenantal living. The law given to Moses is not only about how to be in relationship with God, but also with one another. The body is not to be abused, or used as a commodity, but to be respected. The prophetic tradition upholds the notion of attending well to bodies, as prophets continually call for economic justice. In the New Testament, Paul's words about the body do not discount the Song of Songs; they are, in a sense, the necessary reply to the love poems. The apostle teaches us that the human body is nothing less than the temple of the Holy Spirit, a gift from God (1 Cor. 6:19). Loving partners are to belong to one another solely, remaining constant and faithful to one another and to God (I Cor. 6:13–18; 7:2–4). The body is to be honored.

We see this truth in the being of Jesus himself. God so honored the human body that God's very self took it on—Christ, the Word made flesh (John 1:14). We can even go so far as to say that the incarnate Christ experienced his own divinity within his embodied, physical self. "Who touched my clothes?" he wondered aloud when he felt power go out of him in the middle of a crowd. Although the disciples mocked him for asking such a ridiculous question—who *hadn't* touched him in that jostling mob?—Jesus knew that something profound and significant had taken place, because he felt it within his own body. In the same way, the woman who had been hemorrhaging for twelve years knew it as well; in that instant "she felt in her body that she was healed of her disease" (Mark 5:29). Both of them knew in their bodies, before they knew in their minds, that there had been an encounter with divine power. She knew she had been healed. He knew that through his own body healing had been given to another.

And then of course, there was the eating. Jeff Smith, the Methodist minister known as the Frugal Gourmet, noted that, in the Bible, food talk is God talk. The word "faith" is used about 275 times in the Bible—but the verb "to eat" is used some 800 times! Smith pointed out that "Jesus never says, 'Behold, I stand at the door and knock. If you open the door, I will enter and discuss existential theology with you.' No. Jesus says, 'I will sup with him.'"[14]

Jesus was always eating. He invited himself to people's homes. Someone or other was always giving a dinner party for him. He performed his first miracle at a wedding reception, turning plain old water into the best vintage anyone had ever tasted. He hosted a picnic for more than five thousand one day, and a few days later turned around and did it all again. When he raised Jairus's daughter from the dead, the first thing he suggested was that they find something for the girl to eat. He ate the Passover meal with his disciples and then, later, after he was raised, asked them if they had any fish. On the way to Emmaus, he broke bread with two disciples and they witnessed a miracle, the risen Christ himself. It wasn't just the food that Jesus valued—it was the eating together. He knew that when bodies are fed, spirits are also nourished—that it is around a table where relationships human and divine are forged and strengthened. It was, and is, around a table that Jesus still gathers his body to eat.

Around that table, Jesus is our host and our companion. In Latin, "companion" (or *companio*) makes reference to bread; *com* means with, and *panis* means bread. A companion, then, is one who breaks bread with you. When Jesus was made known to the disciples in the breaking of the bread, he was, quite literally, their companion.[15]

In becoming one of us, Jesus, the One, becomes part of the many. Because of this One, we who are many are also united in him, for we were "born, not of blood or of the will of the flesh or of the will of man, but of God" (John 1:13). Paul helps us understand this as well: "For just as the body is one and has many members, and all the members of the body, though many, are one body, so it is with Christ. For in the one Spirit we were all baptized into one body—Jews or Greeks, slaves or free—and we were all made to drink of one Spirit" (1 Cor. 12:12–13). Baptized into Christ's body, we who are many become part of the One.

Because we are members of the body of Christ—that is, because our very bodies are members of Christ's own body—what we do with our bodies matters (1 Cor. 6:12–20). How we treat our own bodies matters; how others treat our bodies matters; how we treat the bodies of others is of utmost importance. Or, to say it another way, along with blessing and delight come profound ethical implications.

Ethical Implications of the Biblical Understanding of the Body

Certainly the biblical understanding of the body insists on sexual morality—that is, on the use of the body sexually in ways that honor the self and others. And yet sexual morality is only the beginning of the ethical implications that grow from an understanding of how the Bible views the body. To live out the biblical view of the body is to respect the body, yes, and also to feed bodies, to minister to bodies in need of healing, and to pay attention to the needs of the poor.

The last chapter of John's Gospel begins with a simple fishing scene. Peter and some of the other disciples had been at it all night, and to no avail—not one fish lay in the bottom of their boat. It was just after sunrise when they heard a man calling out to them from the beach. He could tell, somehow, that they hadn't caught anything, and so he suggests they put the net down on the other side of the boat. One can only imagine the eye-rolling going on in that fishing vessel, but what did they have to lose? In an instant the net was full of fish, filled to overflowing, so jammed with the squiggly silver things that they couldn't even haul it up into the boat. That was a clear sign for the beloved disciple; "It is the Lord!" he says to impetuous Peter, who proceeds to jump into the water and swim to shore.

By the time the rest of the men do the hard work of getting the boat and the bulging net to shore, Jesus has a fire going. He tells them to bring him some of their catch, and he adds it to the fish he's already got cooking over the fire. "Come on," he says, "have breakfast." And he feeds them well with fresh fish and bread. Of course their spirits are full too—the risen Christ has just come upon them! But Jesus will not let a disembodied spiritual experience be enough; their bodies must be fed too. As we have already noted, it seems that there is something in the eating together that matters. Furthermore, John's language leads us to conclude that there is a connection between our regular meals and the eucharistic meal—between breakfast on the beach and supper at the Table, with the bread and wine we share in worship. "Jesus came and took the bread and gave it to them," John says (John 21:13), echoing the language of the holy meal, feeding them with fish and bread, and also with himself. After they've eaten, Jesus tells them to do the same—"Feed my sheep." The ultimate sign, of course, of how seriously the Bible takes the body is in Jesus' own words at the Passover table. He breaks bread and gives it to them, saying, "Take, eat; this is my body." He pours wine and offers them the cup, saying, "This is my blood of the covenant" (Matt. 26:26, 28). Christians who take the Bible seriously must necessarily take the body seriously, coming to Christ to be fed, feeding one another as well as those who may not be gathered at the same table.

In Jesus' ministry of healing we see yet another facet of how important the body is. Sometimes with a word, sometimes with a touch, he restores the ability to walk to a paralyzed man, or stops a woman's bleeding and gives her back her life. He rubs spit and dirt into the eyes of one who cannot see, restoring sight. He touches the impure and the unclean so that they may be whole in every way. He sends his disciples out to do the same.

In just this way, Jesus is consistently concerned with how his disciples attend to those in distress; for in ministering to the needs of the body we do his work. Consider, for instance, his teaching about the judgment of God near the end of Matthew's Gospel. All the nations will be gathered before Christ, who will say,

> "Come, you that are blessed by my Father, inherit the kingdom prepared for you from the foundation of the world; for I was hungry and you gave me food, I was thirsty and you gave me something to drink, I was a stranger and you welcomed me, I was naked and you gave me clothing, I was sick and you took care of me, I was in prison and you visited me. . . . Truly I tell you, just as you did it to one of the least of these who are members of my family, you did it to me." (Matt. 25:34–36, 40)

One cannot be faithful to Jesus without tending to the bodies of his sisters and brothers.

The miracle of it all is that when we are faithful in this way, Christ meets us there. Some twenty-five years ago, a colleague of mine was teaching at a seminary in New Jersey and serving on the Committee on Social Witness Policy for the newly united Presbyterian Church (U.S.A.). Also on the committee was an Atlanta pastor who, when the committee met in his city, took them to his church. He told them about the night shelter for homeless men that the church helped to sponsor, and also about the relatively new foot clinic they had begun.

The clinic had begun by accident. A woman named Ann Connor, a member of another Atlanta church, drove a van downtown one evening to pick up men who would be guests in the shelter housed at her church. She tells the story this way:

> That evening, as usual, there were more fellows waiting than we could accommodate. One of them for whom there was no room caught my eye because he was limping. Later that night, I called my husband, who was out of town, and told him what had happened. We agreed that if the man was there the next evening, we would bring him to our home.
>
> Sure enough, I found Eugene and brought him back to the house. As we were sharing supper, I told him I was a nurse and asked him why he was limping. He explained that the badly-fitting dress shoes he was wearing had cut into the skin under both ankles and forced him to be treated at a local hospital for blood poisoning. However, the hospital had no other shoes to offer him when he was discharged, so the wounds were re-opening. Reminding him that I was a nurse, I asked him whether I might examine his feet. With shy reluctance, he finally agreed. I got a basin of warm water, some soap and towels and sat down in front of him as he slowly took off his shoes and socks. I winced when I saw the two-inch gashes under each ankle as he lowered his feet into the water.

Ann bathed his feet, anointed them with salve, and bandaged his wounds. She gave him clean socks and a pair of soft slippers. That night, the foot clinic was born. Ann soon began a weekly clinic at her church, and the practice spread to another Atlanta congregation.[16]

When my friend heard this story, she immediately thought, "Why, this is sacramental!" Jesus commanded it, and these people were doing it. She wished she could be part of it. When, a decade later, she found herself called to teach at a seminary in Atlanta, she immediately went to that church and volunteered for the clinic.

She found that it was, indeed, sacramental. "Those guys are a means of grace to me, in a trustworthy way," she says, describing what it is like to bathe and treat the feet of men who walk the pavement all day, every day. "It's like being at the table; I can trust there will be grace there. No matter how tired or how busy or how much I don't want to go—I know that when I get there it will be transforming." Christ, it seems, is already there, pouring out grace with abandon, mediated through water and soap and lotion and one body's caresses of another.[17]

By now it should be clear that this is no disembodied faith. If Jesus shows us this in life, he also shows us in death. The one who was born of a woman took on a human body, ministered to bodies in need, even laid down his own that his body might be raised to new life—and with his, ours. "Listen,

I will tell you a mystery!" exclaims Paul. "We will not all die, but we will all be changed, in a moment, in the twinkling of an eye, at the last trumpet. For the trumpet will sound, and the dead will be raised imperishable, and we will be changed" (1 Cor. 15:51–52). The death and resurrection of Christ— along with the death and resurrection of all Christians—is not just about the resuscitation of a good person with good ideas. It's about the redeeming of all things bodily, the completion of the whole creation. In life and in death, bodies matter. They carry within them the memories of all that God has done and the hope of what God will do. "In Christ salvation itself comes to light in a body," says Nathan Mitchell, and so our own bodies are destined for grace and united not only with Christ, but also with one another, as we share in his resurrection.[18] This relationship between our present bodies and our future resurrection bodies points to the ethical use and treatment of our bodies, and each other's bodies, in the present; in the words of N.T. Wright, "What Christians presently do with their bodies matters, matters eschatologically."[19] In life and in death, we belong to God—mind, soul, body.

For the Sake of the World

We have seen that in worship we are constituted as Christ's own body because we have shared in his baptism. We are bound to one another by that shared ritual, made members of one another and of Christ himself. We are sustained as the body of Christ by what we receive at the table of the Word and the table of the Meal. And we are sent out to be Christ's own body in the world. "Be what you see. Receive what you are," Augustine once proclaimed, exhorting his hearers to take the bread, the body of Christ, and to be that bread for others as they go out to live and work in the world.[20] Gathered in worship as the one body of Christ, our bodies are washed and blessed and fed, that we might be scattered, ourselves bread for a hungry world. Samuel Torvend explains that "the fullness of the body is alive in the gathering of individual bodies united in the local assembly." It is here, in this assembly, that God works through

> a series of real, flesh-and-blood things rooted in experience but reinterpreted, transfigured, by the Spirit's breath: a *common story,* the *water of life*, and *food and drink;* that is the proclamation of the gospel and the enactment of that gospel in baptism and the Eucharist. Or we might say it this way: The Spirit, the breath of life, animates the body with reading from a book, a washing in water, and the sharing of a meal. . . . This is to say that these actions possess a dynamic movement through which the body—the

local assembly—is continually *awakened to faith in God* and *love for the neighbor in need.*[21]

What happens when we gather as the body of Christ, then, is not for our sakes only, but for the sake of the world. As Aidan Kavanagh once put it, "The Sunday liturgy is not the Church assembled to address itself. The liturgy does not cater to the assembly. [Rather], it summons the assembly to enact itself for the life of the world."[22] We come together as Christ's body to be reminded, to be formed, to be changed, to be washed and anointed and blessed, to be fed and encouraged and empowered. Not just so we can go away happy and filled, but so that, having been met by Christ in our midst, we may be Christ for others. Samuel Torvend explains it further: "The assembly—the body—is, in the end, *not* the center. The center is God graciously sending Christ among us in word and sign so that the Christian assembly might go forth to offer its life in prophetic service to this complex, enchanting, and troubled world."[23]

Sara Miles's story is helpful here too. She describes how she eventually became a deacon in the Episcopal Church and began assisting with the Eucharist on Sunday mornings. On many such days, after the worship service, she would trade her alb for her bright yellow St. Gregory's food pantry apron. Circulating among the parishioners while they sipped coffee and enjoyed one another's fellowship, she would offer the remaining eucharistic bread. "More Jesus?" she would ask politely, and then she would mention that the Eucharist continued on Fridays, at the food pantry. "Same table," she would say. "Come feed and be fed."[24] She made the connection clear between the two tables of feeding—the eucharistic table and the pantry table—where the body of Christ was broken and shared.

Acknowledging the embodied nature of our worship, then, is for our sakes, yes, but ultimately it is for the sake of the world. For in claiming our bodiliness, and in honoring the ways that God is mediated to us through our bodies, we are confronted with the realization that as Christians we are compelled to honor the bodies of others, too. Hunger is not an acceptable state; torture cannot be tolerated; there is no room for sexual abuse. We can no longer discriminate because of the color or shape or nationality of a body. We cannot continue to pollute and desecrate the body of the earth. Theologians Andrea Bieler and Luise Schottroff argue persuasively that what we do as the gathered body of Christ is, in fact, about everything:

> The Eucharistic life is about the real stuff: bread and hunger, food and pleasure, eating disorders and global food politics, private property and the common good. The Eucharistic life is about the real stuff in the light of

sacramental permeability. It is about holiness and resurrection; it is about gift exchange, sustainability, and the economy of grace. When we share the holy meal together, when we bring our gifts to the table, when we intercede for the world, when we collect money, and when we give thanks we are entering the realm of eschatological imagination.[25]

Furthermore, they assert that "the body is at the heart of the Eucharistic celebration." What we proclaim and enact grows out of the many-layered understandings of the body in Christian life, and we are propelled to reflect these understandings in every facet of our life in the world. In preaching, in praying, in singing, in washing, in eating and drinking our bodies are gathered and sent. What our bodies do in worship becomes the pattern for what our bodies do in the world, for they are "sacred places through which God acts in the world"[26]—proclaiming good news, interceding for others, praising in all circumstances, showing grace, sharing mercy, doing justice, and in all things giving thanks.

Embodied Worship

If bodies are essential to faithful discipleship, they are also key to faithful worship. "Scripture is replete with references to worshipers using their bodies in approaching God," Jeffrey Mackey reminds us. "Moses removed his shoes, Abraham bowed low when his indescribable visitors approached, David danced before the ark and Daniel faced Jerusalem to pray."[27] When the first Christians gathered for worship, they too brought their bodies, their whole selves. They went to the river to be baptized, that their bodies might be washed in living water. They came together on the first day of the week to tell and retell their shared stories. They stood up to pray, remembering as they rose that Christ's body rose up after his death. And they ate together, breaking bread—the body of Christ—to share among themselves and to take to those who could not be present. Those who were able gave alms for the bodily needs of the poor. From the beginning, Christian worship has been an embodied event. In fact, as Nathan Mitchell asserts, "the human body is . . . more elemental than consciousness itself"; in baptizing and communing, in standing to sing and kneeling to pray, in processing down aisles and laying on hands, we "write the history of [our] relation with God on [our] bodies."[28]

"The human body . . . is intrinsically polyphonic; it speaks several languages simultaneously, just as liturgy and ritual do," states Mitchell.[29] Aidan Kavanagh has framed the same idea in terms of the verbal and nonverbal components of liturgy. The verbal components include, of course, prayers, acclamations, hymns and psalms, Scripture readings, sermons, blessings and dismissals, and so forth. The nonverbal components include elements such as silence—"not the embarrassed, barren, uncontrolled lack of sound which occurs when things break down and no one knows what to say or do," but rather silence that "is purposeful, pregnant, and controlled—the thunderous quiet of people communicating that which escapes being put into mere words." And then there are processions, gestures, and sounds like chanting or instrumental music or the ringing of bells. There are things to be seen and things to be smelled and people to be touched.[30] One begins to see how without the body—our bodies, our bodies together—there would be no worshiping.

We already know this. To truly worship is to bring our whole selves, and it is in worshiping with our whole selves that we are formed as disciples of Jesus Christ. When I come forward to receive bread with my hands held open before me, I come as one hungry to receive grace. I approach the table with so many other hungry people, and in doing so I am shaped, reminded of our utter dependence on God. When I dip my fingers into the baptismal font and trace a cross on my forehead—or better yet, when someone else does—I am reminded in my body that I have been claimed by a God who will not let me go, and empowered for whatever task to which I am called. When I go forward to lay hands on one for whom we pray, I feel my body practically vibrate with the sense that I am part of something so much bigger than myself, and that we are connected to one another and to God, not just through the things we know or believe, but through this remarkable praying thing we do together. We remember things in our bodies; we are shaped by what our bodies do in worship, made disciples of the One who put his body in our midst—and allowed his body to be broken, for our sakes.

The body of Christ gathers, then, to worship, because whenever two or three of us are gathered, there Christ promises to be. The body of Christ gathers to worship because we cannot constitute a body if we insist on going this alone. The body of Christ gathers to use all the languages we have at our disposal—verbal and nonverbal—in order to speak truth the best we know how and to act out with our very bodies that truth that goes far beyond what our words can say.

It follows, then, that those of us who have been called forth from the body to lead worship cannot respond faithfully to that call unless we bring our whole selves to the task. Watching and listening, praying and preaching, baptizing and breaking bread and pouring wine, anointing with oil, laying on hands, moving before and among the people, raising hands in blessing—in all of it, we bring our full beings, trusting that God, through the power of the Holy Spirit, will use our fragile frames to enable the people to pray.

For Further Reading

Andrea Bieler and Luise Schottroff. *The Eucharist: Bodies, Bread, and Resurrection.* Minneapolis: Fortress Press, 2007.

Louis-Marie Chauvet. *The Sacraments: The Word of God at the Mercy of the Body.* Collegeville, MN: Liturgical Press, 2001.

Bruce T. Morrill, ed. *Bodies of Worship: Explorations in Theory and Practice.* Collegeville, MN: Liturgical Press, 1999.

Chapter 3

Eyes and Ears

Attending

*E*udora Welty was a little girl when her parents bought their first automobile. As driving machines were still something of a novelty, one of their neighbors was often invited to go along on the family's Sunday afternoon ride. While Eudora's father drove, her mother would sit in the back with her companion, and young Eudora would settle in between them. As soon as the car got going, she would issue the command: "Now talk." And talk they did.

> There was dialogue throughout the lady's accounts to my mother. "I said" . . . "He said" . . . "And I'm told she very plainly said" . . . "It was midnight before they finally heard, and what do you think it was?"
> What I loved about her stories was that everything happened in scenes. I might not catch on to what the root of the trouble was in all that happened, but my ear told me it was dramatic. Often she said, "The crisis had come!"[1]

At a tender age, the girl who would become a famous author had begun to learn her craft. She listened for stories wherever she was, and these stories enabled her to see.

> Long before I wrote stories, I listened for stories. Listening for them is something more acute than listening to them. I suppose it's an early form of participation in what goes on. Listening children know stories are there. When their elders sit and begin, children are just waiting and hoping for one to come out, like a mouse from its hole.[2]

One can say the same thing about the attentive presider (and, certainly, preacher). In the events of the world, in the day-to-day comings and goings, and in worship itself, we are always listening and watching.

This is nothing new; humans have been this way for centuries. Nathan Mitchell writes of the Cistercians, whose liturgy was sung in monastic churches constructed so exactly "that a pin dropped in the church's nave produces a full set of harmonic overtones." When the monks sang, "the walls quite literally breathed in speech and sound, vibrated with the pitches of rising and falling voices. Song set the building in motion." Perhaps this is why, Mitchell muses, St. Bernard thought that if we are to see God, we must first hear.

> "You should know," he told his monks in a chapter sermon, "that the Holy Spirit educates hearing before leading you to vision. 'Listen my child,' says the Spirit, 'and see.' Why are you straining to see? First it is necessary to lend the ear. Hearing will restore vision to us if our attention is devout, faithful and vigilant. For only hearing attains the truth, since only hearing perceives the Word."
>
> For the early Cistercians, ascetic austerity was balanced by sensual singing, by the skin's recognition that God is known in the marrow before being known in the mind. For them, sound became light and food, charging the body with energy and infusing it with knowledge.[3]

So we learn to be presiders by first learning to listen and to see, that is, learning to attend.

Glimpses of the Kingdom

This sort of attentiveness does not just happen; we must be intentional about it. In one sense, attending means simply noticing what is going on around us and deriving meaning from it. In a deeper sense, however, attending is about seeing through different lenses than the rest of the world. Aidan Kavanagh once opined that "we have lost . . . our ability to see," and perhaps he is right. Rather than seeing the world through the prism of Christian hope, we see the world the way consumer culture would have us see it; in other words, Christians begin to see the way everyone else does. As a result, worship "slips from being a rich, new, countercultural way of seeing and becomes a tertiary ecclesiastical form of entertainment for Sunday mornings." The liturgy is bland, even boring; the preacher may be sincere, but few apprehend it; those who gather around the table disperse without anyone having been changed. Kavanagh's diagnosis is pointed: "The problem is illustrated not by the fact that Christians do not find anything nice to say about the Trinity, but that it never occurs to them to say anything eschatological about the beauty of Elizabeth Taylor [or Angelina Jolie]. Meanwhile, the liturgy slips into being little more than a prolix commercial for a dry 'spiritual' product delivered by a statisticalized system of 'pastoral services.'"[4]

Kavanagh's indictment is stinging, but he is speaking to the heart of what ails the church in North America in the twenty-first century. We have lost sight of what God intends for the world, for we have forgotten how to proclaim it, and enact it, in a way that keeps alive the vision of God's coming reign. In worship, what we proclaim in word and deed is something that together we see, and it forms us in the most profound way. And so, the way we lead worship matters; we are stewards of that eschatological vision and servants of the whole body.

My husband and I spend our summers on the Eastern Shore of Maryland, near the town of Cambridge. On a corner where three streets merge is a little spot where folks can get a bite to eat. The name of the restaurant is spelled out on the window in stick-on letters, "Doris Mae's," and there's a big air conditioner hanging out over the front door. Tourists are not sure whether it is a good idea to go in or not, but the locals know it should not be missed. The food is good, but that is not the main draw. It is the atmosphere, and the atmosphere has everything to do with Doris Mae herself.

Doris Mae died at the age of seventy-four, after running her restaurant for twenty-nine years, serving breakfast and lunch six days a week. Writing about her life, columnist Jim Duffy describes what made the place special:

> Credit for that goes to Doris Mae herself of course. Physically, she was a tiny little thing, but she carried herself in a way that communicated great reserves of strength and joy. She had that broad, bright smile and a big voice, both raspy and cheerful. In busy stretches, she'd work the grill like a dancer, pivoting and flipping and reaching and dipping without missing a beat in the banter between regulars on nearby barstools.

It was not only Doris Mae herself that was remarkable, though; it was also the people she drew to her.

> The mix of customers she brought together every morning was really striking, a we're-all-in-this-together mix of races and classes and professions. On any given morning in Doris Mae's joint, you might see lawyers, barbers, hunters, painters, beauticians, florists, politicians, real estate agents, watermen, homeless guys, and interior designers . . . all trading barbs and gossip and greetings in a veritable symphony of small talk.
>
> I found it pretty much impossible to leave Doris Mae's without a smile on my face. . . . Her place was the real deal.[5]

Mr. Duffy may not use the language of the "kingdom of God" when he describes what happened at Doris Mae's, but he could have. When viewed through the lens of Christian hope, the scene is a foretaste of the heavenly banquet, the coming reign of Christ, where everyone is gathered around the same table, joy abounds, and the barriers that divide us crumble to dust.

It is a matter of training ourselves to see. When the vision of the reign of God is kept before us Sunday after Sunday, we recognize it when we see it, and it makes us want to be part of it. And when we do not see it, it makes us want to create the scene ourselves—both in worship and in the world.

Sometimes the seeing happens to us. In her exquisite memoir, *An American Childhood*, Annie Dillard describes the Sunday morning when she saw something without meaning to. She was a teenager at the time, full of summer camp love for Jesus and utter disdain for the upper-class congregation where her parents dropped her off for worship each week. There came a day when she was chagrined to find that it was a Communion Sunday. She groaned inwardly; she had managed to avoid Communion for years, the long dreary service that seemed interminable. But she was stuck, and there was nothing to do but wait it out.

She watched as the well-dressed ushers passed around sterling silver trays bearing tiny cut-crystal glasses, each with half an ounce of grape juice, and other trays with perfectly cubed white bread. She scoffed inwardly at the presumed piety of these wealthy people in their furs and hats; she glanced sideways at the boys she'd seen at a dance the night before. Then suddenly it hit her. These people were all praying. Even the boys.

> Dan lowered his hands and leaned back slowly. He opened his eyes, unfocused to the high, empty air before him. Wild Jamie moved his arm; he picked up a fistful of hair from his forehead and held it. His eyes fretted tightly shut; his jaws worked. Robert's head lay low on his outstretched sleeves; it moved once from side to side and back again. So they struggled on. I finally looked away.[6]

She had no idea "when this praying developed." She looked down over the balcony rail at the adults below. Even they seemed to be concentrating; surely they were not praying, too. She knew these people—their love for their country clubs and summer parties, their hate for labor unions and laziness. But there they were. The Communion trays had disappeared, and the people were left, stilled. One young father rested his head on two fists propped on his knee. The men's heads were all bowed, the women's too, except for a few who were tilted back. It seemed that people were scarcely breathing. "I was alert enough now to feel, despite myself, some faint thin stream of spirit braiding forward from the pews," Dillard writes.

Its flawed and fragile rivulets pooled far beyond me at the altar. I felt, or saw, its frail strands rise to the wide tower ceiling, and mass in the gold mosaic's dome. The gold tesserae scattered some spirit like light over the cavernous room, and held some of it, like light, in its deep curve. Christ drifted among floating sandstone ledges and deep absorbent skies. There was no speech nor language. The people had been praying, praying to God.[7]

[handwritten margin note: How were they changed?]

It was a baffling vision for the young Dillard, but one, clearly, that she never forgot. Something, or Someone, had caused her to see.

Watching Communion in my own congregation has sometimes caught me by surprise as well. People stream forward for a hunk of bread and a taste of wine; they move like one organism, this body of Christ. They come forward hungry, they come to receive a blessing. They move slowly down the aisle with their walkers, and they come carried in their fathers' arms. The teenagers come in all of their wonderful bold frailty. Many of us are white, some of us are black, or Indian, or Chinese. Some of us are wealthy, and some are politically influential; some of us sleep on the streets or stay at halfway houses. Some of us are successful, and some of us are wrestling with demons. We all come forward with hands outstretched, acknowledging in our very movement our deep hunger for God. Christ is made present not only in the tasting of bread and wine, but also in the seeing.

The seeing is not always a comfort, however; it can also come with the shock of challenge. One bright and promising seminary student tells the story of coming to chapel, practically desperate for the Eucharist. It has been a hard week, full of brokenness and chaos, and she comes to chapel because she just needs to be fed. She waits tiredly and dazedly through the sermon, eager only for that taste of grace. Finally the time for Communion comes, and she makes her way down the aisle, only to realize that the one who will serve her bread, and the one who will serve her wine, are both people she does not like. At all. And they do not like her either. They were people she had once hurt, and they had hurt her too. And then it dawns on her that not only does she need bread and wine, she also needs bread and wine from these people. This is the healing and strengthening she needs most, and it gives her a glimpse of the kingdom breaking in.[8]

In worship and in the world, if we are watching, God actually changes how we see and sets before us a vision of something even better than we had imagined. As William Seth Adams puts it,

With eyes attuned to justice, we see here something suggestive of the Reign of God, a time and place where all are invited to eat, welcomed at the table, given equal portion with indifference as to personal characteristics; a time and place where social consideration marks the occasion, where physical accommodation is exercised as appropriate and necessary, where kindness and generosity are the overarching graces.[9]

The task of attending, then, is multilayered. We listen for stories and the scenes they evoke, so that we see what is going on in the world. We watch what is happening around us, attentive to what God may be doing. We go from day to day, alert for what God might show us, and how we might be changed.

Sometimes God changes us by changing the way we see. In describing the variety of people who emerged to help with St. Gregory's Food Pantry, Sara Miles explains that they came from all sorts of places. The volunteers were church ladies and junkies and street people. They were more than volunteers, actually—they became a community in which people could see all kinds of different folks working and "could imagine themselves needed."

> We had homeless guys and women with missing teeth and a couple who only spoke Tagalog come join us; a transsexual with a thick Bronx accent, some teenagers, an ancient Greek woman from across the street, and a dapper man from St. Gregory's choir who came and played the accordion during the pantry. They were all people who, like me, had come to get fed and stayed to help out. Who, like me, took that bread and got changed. We were all converting: turning into new people as we rubbed up against each other.
>
> The transformation amazed me. I'd think about it as I unpacked the food: blushing red potatoes and curly spinach and ripe peaches that grocers had discarded, and that instead of trash were feeding people. Once I picked up a huge grapefruit and showed it to a volunteer from St. Gregory's. "That's the stone the builders rejected," I said, quoting Scripture aloud with only a twinge of embarrassment. I could see, now, how we were like that, too: the volunteers, and the families who came for groceries. Each of us, at some point, might have been rejected for being too young, too poor, too queer, too old, too crazy or difficult or sick; in one way or another, cracked, broken, not right. But gathered around the Table in this work, we were becoming right together, converted into the cornerstone of something God was building.[10]

It is another vision of the reign of God, acted out by a ragtag bunch of people who find themselves transformed into a community. And in the process of doing that work together, they find that their vision has changed. "'Seeing' actions of communal care and justice, gestures of humility and respect, postures of serenity and enacting them"—all this is central to forming Christians liturgically for the life of discipleship, insists Adams.[11] What we see and enact in worship shapes us for our action in the world; and while we are at work in the world, the Spirit deepens our understanding of that vision of the reign of God that fuels us in the first place. Our sight changes, and we see more; as a result, our prayers are made, both by the words of our mouths and the work of our hands. What we see and hear in worship, then, enables us to apprehend more fully the mystery of God—in the sanctuary and on the street—and allows us glimpses of grace.

Learning to See

One of the first things humans learn to do is to notice things. When my older son, Nate, was first learning to talk, he would point to every truck he saw on the road and gleefully proclaim, "Gruck!" Soon he began to notice that some trucks were bigger than others; about those he would crow, "Gruck gruck!" Noticing, along with playing, is the work of children.

Somehow, as we grow up, we lose the knack for noticing unless we cultivate it as a practice. Outside my office hangs a trio of photographs taken by my younger son, Dan, who is doing just that. Walking through a park in Paris, he spotted an old man who had become friends with birds, and he started shooting pictures. In the first photo, the man's hand is extended, and one bird is perched on a finger. The second photo shows another bird ready to alight, and in the third, both birds have just taken flight. To the casual observer, the pictures show an old man and some sparrows. To the eye practiced in attending, however, the photographs reveal an intricate dance of intimacy between one human being and the creatures with whom he has cultivated a relationship.

To practice this sort of seeing means that we make ourselves open to revelation. Perhaps one of the most famous examples is that of Thomas Merton's epiphany on a street corner:

> In Louisville, at the corner of Fourth and Walnut, in the center of the shopping district, I was suddenly overwhelmed with the realization that I loved all these people, that they were mine and I theirs, that we could not be alien to one another even though we were total strangers. It was like waking from a dream of separateness, of spurious self-isolation in a special world, the world of renunciation and supposed holiness. The whole illusion of a separate holy existence is a dream. Not that I question the reality of my vocation, or of my monastic life: but the conception of "separation from the world" that we have in the monastery too easily presents itself as a complete illusion. . . . We are in the same world as everybody else, the world of the bomb, the world of race hatred, the world of technology, the

world of mass media, big business, revolution, and all the rest. . . . This sense of liberation from an illusory difference was such a relief and such a joy to me that I almost laughed out loud. . . . To think that for sixteen or seventeen years I have been taking seriously this pure illusion that is implicit in so much of our monastic thinking. . . . I have the immense joy of being man, a member of a race in which God himself became incarnate. As if the sorrows and stupidities of the human condition could overwhelm . me, now I realize what we all are. And if only everybody could realize this! But it cannot be explained. There is no way of telling people that they are all walking around shining like the sun.[12]

Noticing, then, is not just for its own sake. It changes us. Merton's vision showed him a whole new way of understanding his life as a monastic; what he saw revealed his connectedness to all people. Far from being separate, or apart, he realizes that he is part of the vast, joyful, heartbreaking web of humanity, and he is never quite the same.

Nathan Mitchell has written compellingly about how what we see changes us, particularly with respect to beauty. He describes the experience of the German poet Rainer Maria Rilke, as he studied a sculpture of Apollo and discovered that the statue was, in fact, looking at him. "In its presence, Rilke concludes, 'there is no place / that does not see you. You must change your life.' You must change your life! . . . Beauty is thus a greeting, a welcome, a summons, a call to conversion: you must change your life."[13] One might say that Merton's vision of all those people "walking around shining like the sun" was a call to conversion, from one way of understanding his vocation to another. As Mitchell explains, however, when we have a glimpse of beauty—or, one might say, a glimpse of the kingdom—that glimpse shows us something not only of the holy, but also of our own sinfulness. Drawing on the work of Elaine Scarry,[14] Mitchell remarks, "Beauty shows us not only the holy, the unprecedented, and the life-giving; it also reveals our almost limitless human capacity for error and deception, for 'getting it wrong,' for making mistakes."[15]

I remember a Sunday when our church choir sang a gorgeous anthem to an energetic, lilting early American tune, arranged by Alice Parker:

Come and taste along with me
consolation flowing free
from the Father's wealthy throne,
sweeter than the honeycomb.

I'll praise God and you praise God
and we'll all praise God together.

We'll praise the Lord for the work that He has done
and we'll bless His name forever.[16]

As we sang, my eyes fell on a woman whom I see often. She sleeps on the streets and comes to worship most Sundays. She rarely misses a Communion Sunday. So we warbled away about the beauty and blessing of tasting the goodness of God, but there was no bread or wine that day. We sang an invitation to meet Christ, but there was no food on the table. The beauty of the music, the beauty of the (potential) meal shone its light on our error—not only for that woman's sake, but also for all our sakes. We had failed to feed her—we had failed to feed us all.

If some acts of beauty show us what we are getting wrong, some can also show us how we sometimes get it right. One Ash Wednesday our church held a midday service, as we often do on holy days, to accommodate legislators and others from the State Capitol who want to worship at noon. This year there were some other people at this service too. One of our pastors had invited guests from the church's homeless shelter to come. And they did. Forty homeless men filled the pews, along with about twenty-five of Georgia's lawmakers.

When it came time for the imposition of ashes, the pastor put the mark of the cross on the first person to come forward, and then that person turned and marked the next person in line. And that's when it happened. A man who spends his days on the streets took an already grimy thumb and covered it with ash. Then he took it and made the sign of the cross on the forehead of one of Georgia's finest. "Remember that you are dust," he said, "and to dust you shall return." One with no power spoke truth to one with all the power: You and I both will die. You and I have both been claimed by God in baptism. You and I both rely—body, mind, and soul—on nothing but the grace of God. And it happened not once, but over and over again, hand to head, ash to skin, as both the greatest and the least of these acknowledged their common humanity and dependence on God.

It was a beautiful thing, not because there was candlelight flickering or beautiful music playing, not because the people were finely dressed or even entirely clean. It was a beautiful thing because it was a glimpse of the kingdom, the place where boundaries are erased. And it convicted us of all the ways we keep those boundaries in place. Because of what we saw, we heard it in our souls: You must change your life. You must make this a reality, not an anomaly. You must see your sisters and brothers differently from now on, and you must live your life in light of that new vision.

Attending in the Liturgy

Practicing watchfulness in the world around us, and in our daily lives, schools us for attending in the liturgy itself. By being alert to what is going on in the lives of the people assembled, and by paying attention to what is happening during a service of worship, presiders can guide the movement, create space, and respond to the moment, helping to enable the people to participate more fully. "The point of effective presiding," says Don Saliers, "is to allow the ears of the assembly to see, and the eyes of the assembly to hear."[17] Those who lead worship do not perform for the crowd, but enhance the action of the congregation itself. As Saliers puts it, "This is at the heart of all faithful presiding: to enable the experience of life before God, of entering into mystery, praise, and lament, a foretaste of the kingdom of God, of formation in faith, hope, and love in the experience of the assembly."[18]

But how does a presider actually do this? First, by watching and listening. Effective presiding cannot be separated from the pastor's life with and among the people. Those who lead worship must listen to the people—to their sorrows, their temptations, their struggles, their doubts, their joys, and their testimonies. Only by listening to those we serve can we preach the gospel in their context; only by listening can we know how to pray in their midst. It matters that we pay attention to the news, listen to talk on the subway or at the diner, bend an ear to fears confessed on hospital beds or confessions whispered in confidence. We preach a gospel that is broad-reaching and we pray for the world, but we also preach and pray in the midst of a particular group of people in a particular place. The God who was born into a specific time and place in human history gives us an incarnational model of ministry.

If we presume to lead worship and proclaim good news without knowing the people who gather, we keep ourselves at a distance and limit our ability to lead the congregation in any meaningful way. "Ordinarily," says Robert Hovda, "one should not be leading people in an activity as deep and central and personal as their ritualizing about the meaning of their lives unless one has previously known them and served them in a role related to fundamental issues."[19] At one level, of course, we proclaim the gospel that all Christians profess, and we share in rituals in which we all find meaning. And yet, when we know something of the lives of those who have entrusted us with their liturgical life, we enter more deeply into reflection on where God calls us, open ourselves more profoundly to how the Spirit empowers us, and experience together the Christ who is in our midst.

Mark Francis urges Christians to have a "listening heart"—that is, to be willing to listen to, and learn from, the people whom one is serving. In other words, one must be willing to be changed—to have one's own faith deepened, one's own vision broadened. He borrows the term from Peter Schineller, who says that this "listening heart," is "an ability to listen to the call of God as it comes through the tradition, and equally important, an ability to listen to the call of God as it comes through the persons in the situation where one is ministering." Francis further explains that this means "putting the tradition in dialogue with the lives and the experiences of others in order for all involved to see the movement of God's spirit, which is constantly 'making all things new.'"[20]

Sometimes this listening heart makes us more deeply connected to people we know well; sometimes it means encountering folks who are much different from us, and allowing ourselves to be changed by them. I am learning this from some people who come to worship where I do, like the man who joined us one Easter Sunday. It seemed that most of his teeth were gone, and though he looked clean and neat, his sport coat was decidedly too large. My husband was seated in the same pew, and when people passed the friendship pad, he saw the man had written his name in the proper space, and where it said "address" he had written "homeless." From my perch in the choir loft I could see him as he sang all the hymns and recited the creed. I had not seen him before; I have not seen him since. But he was a brother in Christ, there to celebrate the resurrection of Jesus.

During the announcements the pastor explained that a special offering was to be taken that day to benefit the poor and the hungry all around the world. There were envelopes in the pews for the purpose, and when it came time for the offering, he said, we were all to give generously.

The appointed time came, and my husband watched as the man took one of the special envelopes. He did not put any money in, and for a moment my husband wondered if he ought to be giving his money to the man instead of to the special offering. But the man had his own offering to give. On the envelope he wrote, "I love you very much."

His presence, and the presence of others who live life on the streets, in this predominantly middle- and upper-middle-class congregation changes us. We cannot preach and pray as though they are not part of the body! A preacher who sees a person in a knit cap wrapped in a blanket will—or should—make different assumptions about her hearers. The example of the lawyer in the Lexus driving past a beggar on the street suddenly sounds hollow when both the lawyer and the beggar are in the pews. The tirade against materialism sounds different when at least one person in the congregation does not have two nickels to rub together. Even the injunction to go out and feed the poor sounds a little off pitch when the poor are right there in front of you. Because now the "needy" are not out there somewhere; they are in here—they are not they, but we, part of the body.

If we are paying attention, then, we notice who is in our congregations, and their presence cues us how to preach and pray. Yet we are not the only ones who need to learn to pay attention. William Seth Adams instructs us wisely when he says that those of us who lead in worship must not only practice attending, but we must also "enable the community 'to see' and to be thoughtful about what is shown forth." This depends, he says, on expectation: "What is 'seen' or rather 'seeable' depends on the expectations of the 'see-er.' This is not to say that we see what we expect to see—that our seeing causes predictable outcomes—but rather that our expectations inform our ability to see deeply. If we do not expect deeply, we will likely not see deeply." That is, we must not only attend carefully and see deeply ourselves, but we must also enable our congregations to expect to see deeply too.[21]

So, how we do we do that? How do we help our congregations to see? The answer begins rather simply: we pay attention, in a way that makes it clear to anyone watching that we are doing so. In other words, being fully attentive in worship means being seen in that posture. We all know what it looks like when a presider is not attending well. She is fumbling with the pages of her sermon, or scribbling out a prayer while someone else is "on." Or he is making hand signals or mouthing messages to someone in the congregation while the choir sings. When those of us who lead worship persist in doing something other than attending to whatever the action is, we convey to anyone who may be watching that the action is unimportant. But when a presider is attentive to whatever is going on—whether someone is making an announcement, or the children are singing, or a lector is reading Scripture—then others in the worshiping congregation notice that something significant is happening, or, at the very least, they are not distracted by the fidgety presider. "Some presiders affect a slightly dazed look, as if wondering what is coming next," Hovda laments. "Others wear that look quite honestly." He recommends that those types ought not be allowed anywhere near a pulpit or table! For there is too much at stake. "The appearance of the person [in the role of presider] is the most powerful signal the congregation has that the work it is engaged in has some importance, some meaning, some clarity and logic. A presider who looks baffled demoralizes the assembly without uttering a word, whereas one who is confident of the rite and its progression communicates positively with everyone."[22]

To put it another way, the first step in leading others to attentiveness is to know what to do when you are not doing anything. Even when a presider is seemingly idle, what she does with her eyes, hands, and posture leads the congregation. A presider always communicates something—so why not be intentional about what you are communicating? Even when you are "doing nothing," you are actively sharing leadership with another and intentionally attending to what that person is doing in the service. As Hovda puts it, "The presider facilitates, discreetly yields the focus to the one who is operating at a particular moment, guides, prompts when necessary, leads the congregation in attending to the action."[23] Even more, he insists, if the presider does all the parts of the liturgy except those that involve the entire congregation, "we have a kind of liturgical barbarism. Where, then, are the talents and the gifts and the competencies of the community?" In other words, we presiders do not do this work of leading alone; if we do, we are robbing the community of its own richness and communicating that the enabling of worship is best left to professionals.

Another crucial element of attending well is knowing what comes next. In a well-designed worship service, there is an internal logic at work, a movement from one point to the next as the congregation journeys together from a time of gathering to a time of sending. An effective presider carries in his body an understanding of the steps of that journey, and he knows at any moment in the service what will follow. This is crucial in any service, but if the service has any special or unusual elements, it is necessary to think even more carefully through the logistics and sometimes even to practice ahead of time. As Hovda puts it, "A quiet enthusiasm and a conviction about the importance of liturgical action are assets that a presider can neither feign nor do without."[24]

Consider, for instance, the sequence that includes a call to confession, a prayer of confession, a declaration of forgiveness, and a response to the good news. There is a clear progression here: the presider calls people to confess their sin to God, affirming that God waits in mercy to forgive us even before we ask. The tone is serious, then, but also full of promise. The presider looks people in the eye when calling them to confession, because confession is an admission of every human's need for, and dependence on, God, and we are all in this together. The presider anticipates an honest prayer as well as the assurance of grace. The prayer of confession, which might be prayed corporately, is a truth-telling prayer, which makes it both humble and bold. Imagine—we are so sure that God is merciful that we can actually admit our failings to the One who is the judge of all righteousness. If the presider is paying attention at all, the declaration of forgiveness that follows cannot be delivered in a rote or detached manner. This is the good news that is at the heart of the gospel! Because the presider knows the logic—from call and promise, to honest truth-telling, to joyful declaration of God's faithfulness, the people know this grace-filled movement too, and are ready to sing a full-throated expression of praise or call out a hearty "Thanks be to God!" after hearing the good news. The presider will want to take part in this too, and so continues to stand in the same place, participating fully in the action (that is, the singing or the speaking) before returning to his chair or moving to the next part of the service. The presider who attends to the various segments of the liturgy will enable the people to enter into the movement of the service, to intuit that the worship service is not just a jumble of disconnected elements, but a journey in the presence of God.

The presider who is paying attention is also better equipped when things go wrong, which, of course, they will. When the service has been prepared well, and the presider is well aware of the liturgy's moving parts, then she is better able to think on her feet when things don't go as smoothly as planned. As good advice as any comes from (of all places!) the classic cookbook *The Joy of Cooking*. Here is what the authors say about what to do when something goes wrong while entertaining: "If, at the last minute, something does happen to upset your well-laid plans, rise to the occasion. The mishap may be the making of your party. Capitalize on it, but not too heavily. Remember that in Roman times the poet Horace observed, 'A host is like a general: It takes a mishap to reveal genius.'"[25] What works for a dinner party works for liturgy too. When things go wrong, go with the flow, keep your sense of humor, and cover all things with grace.

The attentive presider, then, works with something of an improvisational style. This means not only being prepared, but also cultivating the ability to respond to the unexpected challenges and graces of the moment. Pastor and author Eugenia Gamble tells the story of what happened one Maundy Thursday evening when an unexpected guest arrived in the middle of the service. A scruffy-looking man who looked as though he had spent some time on the streets wandered in and slowly made his way to the front of the sanctuary, where he sank into a pew and looked around with a rather dazed expression on his face. The sermon was coming to a close, and the pastor issued the invitation to the Table.

> The man watched me and, sad truth be told, I had my eye on him, too. When I invited the congregation to come forward to receive the elements, he seemed to look around, unsure. Did he not know what to do? Was he afraid that the gifts of God for the people of God did not include him? One of the saints of our church went to him and invited him forward. He took off his hat and shuffled toward the table. I was offering the bread. "The Body of Christ, the bread of heaven," I said. The shepherding saint who was with him, whispered to him to tear off a piece of bread and dip it in

the "goblet." He did. A big hunk. A worthy hunk. And he stood right there and ate it, chewing loudly and looking me straight in the eye. He gulped. His surprisingly sweet tenor voice lifted from deep somewhere, loud somewhere, "This is so good! So sweet and good." I gulped. My eyes swam with tears. I could hear congregants take their breaths in sharply and almost sing a sigh. "Yes," we thought. "This is so good, so sweet and good." He stood rooted to the spot. Just as I was about to nudge him forward he asked, "May I have some more? I am so hungry."

Suddenly he spoke for us all, all of us rag-tag-bobtailed band of believers whose deep hungers are so rarely met, and we found in that moment a bountiful host and a powerful yearning. "When everyone has had a little," I said. "You may have the rest." "Thank you, Ma'am," he said. I really cried then.

The rest of us received. The elders were served. I savored the bread like manna, like the only thing that stood between me and a brutal desert death. I took him the paten and all during the final prayers, all during the closing hymn, all during the benediction, he sat and ate and said, again and again, "Mmmm, Mmmm, Mmmm. So Sweet. So Sweet."[26]

To have such presence of mind requires a presider who is good at attending— at watching who comes, and knowing what grace looks like.

There are other times when this sort of improvisational spirit can fill a gap. At one summer worship and music conference, the planning team had decided to incorporate a remembrance of baptism into the closing rite of the final service. I gave the charge from the font:

> You who have been born of water
> and anointed with the Holy Spirit,
> go forth from this place,
> following wherever God may lead
> to show forth Christ's light to the world.
>
> And as you go, remember
> that whatever is required of you,
> your baptism is sufficient for your calling.

The preacher gave a blessing, and then dancers came to the font, bearing bowls. Using a pitcher, I dipped water from the font into their bowls, and they went off to various sections of the large sanctuary, using branches to fling droplets of water on the upturned faces and outstretched hands of those who were being sent forth with the reminder that they were the baptized people of God.

I watched from the chancel area as people took part in this joyful closing rite—and then noticed that down in the front there was a whole section of people who were being left out. Due to a logistical glitch, no dancer had been assigned to their section, and so they looked around at everyone else enjoying blessing. Some of them looked up at me, and shrugged and smiled, as if to say, "Oh, well."

I sure was no dancer, and I had no water bowl and no branch, but I did have my pitcher. So I filled it up with water from the font and went to them, flinging water with my hand and practically leaping off the floor to make sure the droplets made it to everyone. I may not have been the most graceful one out there, but now everyone was equally splattered and equally blessed, and we were all joyful because no one was left out.

The effective presider, then, is constantly attending, eyes wide open and ears alert, listening for the community's stories and watching for signs of the inbreaking of God's reign. In fact, it takes all the senses working together—for the presider and for the congregation. Then, says Don Saliers, we can "move beyond either a dull traditionalism, or a new literalism of hyped-up sense experience."[27] And so, having considered what it means to carefully attend with eyes and ears, we turn to the mouth, the instrument of proclamation and prayer.

For Further Reading

Sara Miles. *Take This Bread: A Radical Conversion.* New York: Ballantine Books, 2005.

Eudora Welty. *One Writer's Beginnings.* Cambridge, MA: Warner Books, 1983.

Chapter 4

The Mouth

Voice and Speech

*R*ecent decades have witnessed a remarkable growth in television and other forms of visual media. The vast majority of households in North America own at least one television set, and forms of video communication on the Internet are sprouting up with great frequency. In his thought-provoking book *The Rise of the Image, the Fall of the Word*, Mitchell Stephens makes the case that the image is supplanting the word:

> We know this. Evidence of the growing popularity of images has been difficult to ignore. It has been available in most of our bedrooms and living rooms, where the machine most responsible for the image's rise has long dominated the décor. Evidence has been available in the shift in home design from bookshelves to "entertainment centers," from libraries to "family rooms," or, more accurately, "TV rooms." Evidence has been available in our children's facility with remote controls and joysticks, and their lack of facility with language. Evidence has been available almost any evening in almost any town in the world, where a stroller will observe a blue light in most of the windows and a notable absence of porch sitters, gossip mongers and other strollers.[1]

With our growing infatuation with all things visual, we have seen video replace narrative, and the implication is that our words matter less than they used to. Some will tell you that the time for hearing is past, that it is not speech or sound that compels the contemporary believer or seeker, but vision and sight. Yet not everyone is convinced. Homiletician Richard Lischer minces no words in his commentary on the matter:

> Most of us like to think that we have adapted to the information technology that surrounds us and harnessed it to the needs of the kingdom, but those who are preachers know the true and lively word—so rich in paradox, metaphor,

and narrative, so demanding of community and time for absorption—does not match up well with its digitalized environment.[2]

In fact, Lischer contends, in some "large, successful churches," "members would never dream that the light-shows, videos, and PowerPoint presentations that accompany the Sunday sermon represent a fundamental lack of confidence in the spoken word of God."[3]

What brought this shift? Lischer speculates "that some preachers embrace technology because they recognize that the old communities of memory have broken down. What they may not understand is that the cords of memory have been cut by the very technology they are uncritically adopting. The small community that once faithfully gathered around altar and table is now shopping for a more comprehensive program. What holds many congregations together is not tradition or common experience but a style of consumption and a method of communication."[4]

Others would argue that long before the first projection screens appeared in sanctuaries, we gave up on words. Kathleen Norris points to Thomas Merton, who opined some four decades ago that "people don't want to hear any more words. In our mechanical age, all words have become alike. . . . To say 'God is Love' is like saying, 'Eat Wheaties.'"[5] Like Merton, Norris believes that the language of advertising has become so pervasive as to have numbed the ears of worshipers and eviscerated religious language of its revelatory power.[6] Furthermore, her own experience worshiping in a Presbyterian church (a denomination to which she remains loyal) has caused her astonishment at "the sheer quantity of verbiage. It felt like a word bombardment, and I often needed a three-hour nap to recover. I began to wonder why people in a religion of the Word were so often careless with their words, particularly the words used in worship and biblical translations."[7]

Lischer and Norris point to the need to reclaim attention to language and the power of speech in both preaching and liturgy, and they are not alone. But even before we consider language, we must first turn to that which creates speech: the voice, human and divine. Speaking is a necessarily embodied act, and the voice is an instrument of proclamation and prayer. Effective presiders, then, understand the voice theologically as well as practically, and it is here that we begin.

A Theology of Speech

Speaking is at the core of what it means to be Christian. Or, to put it in the words of Stephen H. Webb, author of *The Divine Voice: Christian Procla-*

mation and the Theology of Sound, "There is . . . a soundscape to Christian theology."[8] The world was brought into being when God spoke (Gen. 1:3). For Christians, God's fullest revelation is in Jesus Christ, the incarnate Word, who was there at the beginning (John 1:1), and his disciples have heard his call to follow. Of course, there is no limit to the manner of ways in which God can speak, whether with or without words. The voice of God thunders (Pss. 18:13; 29:3; Job 40:9), or it sounds like rushing waters (Ezek. 43:2; Rev. 1:9–19). It speaks in words to Moses and the prophets (Exod. 19:19; Deut. 4:12; Isa. 6:8; Ezek. 1:23–25), but Elijah hears God's voice in the silence (1 Kgs. 19:11–17). There is no one sound to God's voice; sometimes God speaks without words or sounds at all. Yet the Bible, argues Webb, "puts a premium on sound as God's most typical choice of a medium for communication, and vocal speech is the form the sound of God most frequently takes."[9]

As beings created in the image of God, "we can speak only because God created us to be hearers of God's Word," Webb insists. "God spoke us into being so that we too might have the joy of sharing in the spoken Word," even to "speak on God's behalf."[10] God, then, is revealed not only in the divine voice, but in the human voice as well, as it echoes the divine voice. Webb puts it well:

> God's voice is holy, but it is less commonly pointed out that a God who speaks is a God who is revealed not only in the divine but also in the human voice. The prophets are revered in the Bible as those called to speak in God's name, since they balance God's deafening demands for justice with God's soft murmurs of mercy. The prophets demonstrate how human voices can mediate the divine plan. All speech, therefore, is endowed with potentially sacred significance. All of us can imitate God's words with our own, by talking each other out of the despair of isolation and into healthy and just relations. The Spirit moves through us like a wind as we exhale sounds into the world. Our power lies in speech too.[11]

In other words, the God who spoke us into being calls forth speech from us as well. The divine voice summons human voices to echo God's own Word, not just in imitation, but also as a way of being in relation with God and God's purposes in the world. To be Christian, in fact, is to hear the Word and then to testify. "So faith comes from what is heard, and what is heard comes through the word of Christ," wrote Paul (Rom. 10:17). "But just as we have the same spirit of faith that is in accordance with scripture—'I believed, and so I spoke'—we also believe, and so we speak" (2 Cor. 4:13).

Before pursuing further this line of thought, it is important to note that members of the deaf culture may take issue with the assertion that Christian faith is dependent on speech. At the most profound level, we must acknowl-edge that God is not limited in the ways God communicates with humans. And neither are humans limited to one way of communication; American Sign Language, which uses gesture rather than sound, is recognized as a lan-guage as complex, expressive, and rich as any other. The primary way we are talking about voice and speech, then, is metaphorical. While we will go on to discuss the use of the human voice and the sacramental nature of speech, the thoughts presented here might apply to both spoken and signed com-munication. What is key is the dialogue that takes place between God and humans and among the people themselves when they communicate with, and about, God.[12]

Thoughtful and effective presiders in worship recognize the theological significance of the voice. Although God is able to communicate without words, and does, the voice is central to the proclamation of the good news. Practically speaking, used well the voice is a powerful tool, not to "create an experience" for worshipers, but to enable them to hear and respond to God's Word—that is, to evoke the people's prayer and their work in the world.

Thomas Troeger draws on the poetry of George Herbert to make this point about preaching in particular. He had returned to Herbert's collection of poems, *The Temple*, after many years, and his eyes fell on two lines that struck him in a way they couldn't have when he was a teenager:

> Resort to sermons; but to prayers most:
> Praying's the end of preaching . . .[13]

These lines led Troeger to consider the ultimate purpose of preaching. "If the end of preaching is prayer," he writes,

> then all preachers need to ask: What kind of prayer does their preaching awaken? I am not suggesting every sermon ought to be about prayer or that every sermon will conclude with the preacher offering a prayer. But rather I am asking: What kind of living relationship with God does preaching nurture over time? Does it nurture the deep, broad relationship with God that is expressed through the extravagant richness of the church's corporate life of prayer?[14]

Troeger goes on to explain that preaching, properly understood, leads people to respond to God through all manner of praying—adoration, confession, supplication, intercession, thanksgiving, and lament. As Troeger puts it, "Homiletics does not start with hermeneutics or rhetoric; it starts with God and our relationship to God and the vast repertoire of human prayer. . . . The end of preaching is prayer. The beginning of preaching is prayer."[15]

What a difference this makes for those who preside and preach. For if preaching—the proclamation of the Word—is to enable people to hear the Word and then respond to God because of the Word, then preaching is dialogical. In other words, preaching is a conversation, and the lines of communication are many. The preacher, in prayer, listens for God as the sermon takes shape throughout the week. Sometimes God speaks directly to the preacher's heart and mind; other times God's answer comes through the voice of the people—in casual conversations, hospital visits, committee meetings, and youth group discussions. When the time for proclamation comes, the people, having prayed for illumination of the Word through the power of the Holy Spirit, listen for God through the words of Scripture and the words of the preacher. They respond to God in kind, through their prayers, their testimonies, and their work in the world. And they respond to the preacher as well, not just with a polite handshake at the church door, but with questions and challenges and insights and tears. To think of preaching in this way keeps preachers from imagining that their main purpose is to dispense wise advice or to tell entertaining stories. It turns them away from the impulse to impart information. Rather, it calls preachers to listen for the voice of God however and wherever it may emerge and then to testify— to bear witness to what they have seen and heard, so that the community might also encounter the living Christ and go out to tell the story.[16]

Speech carries forth not only proclamation, of course, but other forms of liturgical speech as well—invitations and declarations, prayers and blessings. The words we speak in worship are conduits for the divine Word; our very bodies, through our voices, bear forth that Word. And somewhere in the midst of the words and the silences, we encounter the Holy One. That makes our speech sacramental. Like everyday bread and wine, our common words, by a miracle of grace, are transformed so that in our proclamation and our songs and our prayers Christ is made known to us.

The Sacramentality of Speech: Proclamation

The Lord's Day service offers three key moments when the gospel is proclaimed. Most obviously, the reading and preaching of Scripture is the chief proclamatory event. Yet there are two other key events in worship when good news is proclaimed: the declaration of forgiveness and the benediction. Looking at the scope of a service, these might seem like small things, yet these two moments carry the full weight of gospel proclamation, and it matters how they are spoken and enacted, just as it matters how Scripture is proclaimed and preached.

Proclaiming Scripture

In one segment of Thomas A. Kane's remarkable video collection titled *The Dancing Church around the World*, we see the Gospel procession during a worship service at the Poor Clare Monastery in Lilongwe, Malawi.[17] To the accompaniment of spirited drumming and singing, the choir dances in the Gospel book, circling the table several times before opening the vessel in which the book rests. This vessel is a large, round clay pot, wrapped in cloth. The community sees the pot as Mary's womb, which bears the Word for the people. When the pot is unwrapped, and the lid is removed, the book is taken forth and held high, while the people rejoice with ululations. The Word has been born again.

The procession is a vivid, enacted reminder that Jesus is the Word incarnate, and that the Word read and proclaimed in worship is sacramental. Reformed theologian J. J. von Allmen once suggested that "like Mary, 'who receives, clothes with her substance and gives forth to the world, God's eternal Word,' the preacher receives God's word, clothes it in human words, and proclaims to the world God's eternal Word." As Leanne van Dyk points out, this implies "a deep connection between the act of preaching and the incarnate Word of God, Jesus Christ." The human voice and the divine voice are intertwined. "Despite the aspect of a human testimony which it also bears," says von Allmen, "Christian preaching is not simply a meditation on the Word of God. It is a *proclamation* of that Word; it implies a divine miracle." Van Dyk comments wryly that the idea of a sermon as anything miraculous might cause some raising of eyebrows. Yet, she explains, von Allmen isn't talking about the brilliance or skill or wit of the preacher. Rather, "the sermon is, by its audacious claim to be the word of God for the people at this time in this place, an implication of a miracle. The miracle is a faint but, by God's grace, an unmistakable 'incarnation' of Jesus Christ. Fully divine, fully human, yet one God-with-us is the Christian confession of the nature of Christ. The sermon dares make the same claim."[18]

The idea that speech is sacramental is, of course, not a new one. John Calvin saw the word as a means of grace, since Christ is present in the word as in the sacraments. Karl Barth also recognized the sacramentality of preaching, asserting that "real proclamation as this new event, in which the event of human language about God is not set aside, but rather exalted, is the Word of God."[19] On the one hand, this view of the Word as sacramental—of the sacramentality of speech and its conduit, the voice—gives new life to our understanding of preaching. On the other hand, it is also the cause of great trepidation. "Even the most confident preacher can be frozen into homiletical paralysis by Barth's challenge," admits Patrick Willson, going on to quote the theologian: "What are you doing, you, . . . with the word of *God* upon *your* lips?" Indeed. Fortunately, God does not leave us to our own devices. Willson puts it well:

> To name the Word as a sacrament and reflect on the mystery of our human words becoming—by God's grace and appointment—the vehicles of the very Word of God should shock us into an appropriate astonishment, a very good place for preaching to begin. In shocked silence we may surrender glib competence along with our cute stories. Barth's dizzying dialecticism describes our situation: we cannot speak of God; we must speak of God; God insists we speak in our incapacity to speak. Sitting in astonished silence, wondering at the dimensions of the task before us might be exactly what we need to deliver us from consumer pressures to imitate stand-up comics and talk show hosts. Recognizing the Word as sacrament might place in proper perspective those volumes that propose we think of "preaching" as something borrowed from literature or drama. Let us rather name preaching *as* the sacrament of the Word. God has a larger and more profound agenda than the amusement of a gathered congregation. Beginning our work in astonishment reminds us that we are caught up in a larger project than simply "getting up" this week's sermon.[20]

That astonishment leads us to deep and prayerful encounters with God in Scripture, long before we ever step into a pulpit. And, as Willson reminds us, the God who spoke the world into being is speaking still, sometimes even through our own speech.

Even with this perspective in place, how do preachers muster the courage to stand before God's own people and utter a single word? In one church, the fearful caution is etched into the very pulpit itself:

> The pulpit of St. Stephen's Cathedral in Vienna displays an elaborate handrail in which are carved a detailed series of ugly, mythical creatures. The open mouths and oversized snouts of the beasts are there to remind the preacher of his inadequacies as he ascends the stairs. At the very top of the handrail, carved into the pillar that separates the stairs from the open, circular pulpit, stands a dog, jaws open, barking down at the ominous figures. The hellish beasts are not to enter the sacred place. The preacher has been enjoined to leave his sinful self behind as he prepares to speak God's Word.
>
> The medieval artisan has captured in stone the inner tension of all of us who dare to preach. We are aware that the words we speak are human words, formed through reflection both on the Scriptures and on our personal experience of the needs of our community. Looking into the faces of the people who sit before us, we see those who are holier, more intelligent,

and more creative. And yet they wait for us to speak, to preach, to proclaim and witness to the presence of God among us. . . .

We dare to utter that sacred Word because we once heard the voice of Mystery who spoke to Isaiah: "Whom shall I send? Who will go for us?" And we answered with Isaiah, "Here I am; send me."[21] (Isa. 6:8)

We preach because it is called out from us—not because we are skilled or smooth or charismatic or attractive. We preach because it is what God has required from us. From *us*, mortal and imperfect as we are. As Dominican theologian William Hill once said, "We must take seriously the fragility of the *human* situation here." Yet God's own act in history was one of kenosis, self-emptying, and God still means to further the coming of the kingdom "in and through the weak things of the world. And so, paradoxically, God cannot do without the stammering ways in which we strive to give utterance to that Word."[22] Thankfully, then, grace abounds, and God "continues to set apart and sanctify human lips and tongues and words and sermons to call people into the drama of God's saving work."[23]

If we accept this notion that the Word is sacramental—that even *our* words can be sacramental, then we cannot escape the significance of the human voice in proclaiming that Word. Practically speaking, it changes the way presiders, preachers, or lectors approach the reading of Scripture. As Stephen Webb points out, the reading of Scripture ought to be a highlight of worship. In fact, he muses, if we paid more attention "to the dramatic qualities of the Sunday reading of Scripture, there would be less interest in performing actual dramas during worship."[24] In fact, there is plenty of drama in Scripture. One is reminded of the cartoon where one small child, after hearing a particularly colorful story from the Bible during Sunday school, turns to another and says incredulously, "Does anybody else know that stuff is in there?"

At the heart of the matter is this: If we believe Christ is made present in the reading of the Word, we cannot simply go through the motions, unthinking, unmoved, disengaged. Before we approach the pulpit (or lectern or ambo), we must take in the words of the reading, chewing them like bread, making them part of us—so that when the time comes we do not drone through the passage as if nothing particularly significant is going on, but speak as though the words have become, somehow, part of us. This does not mean treating it like readers' theater, intoning the words of Scripture as though we were telling a story to children or narrating a play. The best readers of Scripture know that proclaiming from the Bible is more than just good theater. While elocution and expressiveness are important skills to bring to the task, the best readers do not overdramatize. As Webb puts it,

Good readers try not to deflect attention from the Bible with too much variation in cadence and pitch. They use their regular voices, yet they heighten the sense of purpose in their tone. They speak plainly but seriously, as if the Word of God were written especially for each listener, and each listener will know what to do with it when the reading is done. The reader is delivering a message that is not her own, so she is not free to present it however she wishes. Regardless of how well she understands it, she wants her words to convey some of its urgency and weight.[25]

In other words, those who read Scripture do so not as performers, but as members of the body. We do not act upon the words—the words act upon us, so that we cannot help but proclaim them, not just read them. These words from Scripture aren't just any words; they are holy words, bearers of truth, God's own Word. There is, as Webb says, urgency here—these words matter. In Scripture and sermon we encounter God, the living Word; our own voices carry those words, making them into sound; our very breath brings them to holy speech. Like Mary, we bear the very Word of God in our bodies.

Some speak of this quality as "transparency"—the reader gets out of the way, becoming a vessel for the Word without imposing his or her character or personality upon it. As bearer of the Word, the reader does not call attention to herself, but to the text. Being transparent, however, is not the same as being bland, for our particularity is part of the proclamatory event. The Word sounds different in the voice of an eighty-year-old woman than it does in the voice of an eight-year-old boy, and it should.

Although the act of proclamation is not a theatrical event, there are those who would bring to preaching the skills and sensibilities of the theater, and they have helpful knowledge to share. Jana Childers and Richard Ward, for example, have brought considerable experience and training in performance studies to the homiletical conversation, and their insights help make better preachers.[26] Still, when all is said and done, what makes preaching an event is not only theatrical skill, but also the sacramental nature of the word—the sanctification of speech—that comes not through our own doing, but the work of the Holy Spirit, who imbues our frail and imperfect words that they might show forth something of the divine Word.

Confession and Pardon

In a congregation I once served, a young man told me that for him the high point of every service was the declaration of forgiveness. He was an officer of the church, a faithful worshiper, an attentive husband and father. In other words, he didn't seem any more in need of forgiveness than the rest of us.

Yet he heard gospel in that moment; the promise he depended on, the grace he counted on, was reiterated, unequivocally, each and every week. Knowing that changed how I approached this moment in worship. Even though we speak words of forgiveness every week, they are never perfunctory. They are a matter of death and life.

The first step in knowing how to proclaim forgiveness is to understand why we confess in the first place. If we are honest about it, we have to admit that there are those Sundays when we obediently read the corporate prayer of confession printed in our bulletins and think, "I didn't do that this week," or "I've never done that!" Then, during the time of silent prayer, we hurriedly try to make a respectable list of transgressions to show that we're taking it all seriously. We wonder if we're missing something here, and in fact we might be. For confession is less about compiling a laundry list of our sins and more about the melting of our hardened hearts.

Perhaps the best place to look for instruction on the nature of confession is Psalm 51, the quintessential confessional psalm. In spite of the fact that the superscription of this psalm connects it to the story of David's dalliance with Bathsheba—the one that led to the breaking of fully half of the Ten Commandments—this psalm is not just about needing to be pardoned for particular wrongdoings. Rather, as Old Testament scholar James Mays puts it, it's about "deliverance from the predicament of [ourselves]."[27] In other words, sin is not about laundry lists at all, but about the human condition—and repentance concerns who we are, not just what we've done.

We can tell this, in part, because already, in the first three verses of the psalm, the whole Old Testament vocabulary for sin is used; that is, all the words that mean transgression, iniquity, sin are there. This confession is meant to be comprehensive—it covers all the bases: culpability, rebellion, injury to others, and just general bad behavior.

The psalmist does not stop there, however, but goes on to remind us that we can do no other. "I was born guilty, a sinner when my mother conceived me," goes the lament—not in order to establish the doctrine of original sin, or to warn us about the inherent sinfulness of sex, as has been suggested all too often through the centuries, but rather to acknowledge the truth about who we are: limited creatures, made in the image of God, yes, but not divine at all—people who are utterly dependent on God and in constant need of grace.

We like to pretend that it's otherwise, that we are not so needful of forgiveness. We've come to depend on our own strengths and virtues and talents and gifts, and we are in love with the idea that we can be self-sufficient. In spite of all our talk in the church about things like community and vulnerability, we'd prefer to have as little do to with either of them as possible. We understand all about sin and grace; after all, we are the ones in worship every week. Which may be what makes us most susceptible.

In his classic book *Life Together*, Dietrich Bonhoeffer rather bluntly points out that once we're part of the church, we consider ourselves members of a "pious fellowship [that] permits no one to be a sinner." Everybody must hide their sins—from themselves and from each other—pretending that the need for grace is something that was taken care of a long time ago. In fact, he says, "Many Christians are unthinkably horrified when a real sinner is suddenly discovered among the righteous. So we remain alone with our sin, living in lies and hypocrisy."[28] Bonhoeffer points to the heart of what confession is about: truth-telling. Confession is our unabashed admitting that we need God.

The psalmist asks for "a new and right spirit"—that is, a mind and a will inhabited by God. To pray for that means giving up our illusions that we already possess (or *should* possess) all the strength and wisdom and goodness we need. It means releasing every fear to which we so tightly cling, that we might receive into our open hands the courage and strength we crave. It means telling the truth about our inability to get along, and coming clean about our failure to live out justice in our world, in our communities, and even in our homes, in spite of all the time we spend talking about it. In short, it means allowing our wills to be bent and our hearts to be broken, so that they might be made whole again.

In other words, when it comes to confession and pardon, what sounds like bad news is really very good news. For in spite of our stubbornness and nearsightedness, God waits to pour out mercy upon all who desire it—to gift us with a new and right spirit—that we might be filled with joy. So, then, confession is not about shame, but freedom from it. It is not about losing face, but receiving grace—buckets of it, torrents of it, mercy poured out till we are filled to overflowing—and we cannot help but shout out the good news of God's love.

To proclaim forgiveness after truth-telling is, perhaps, the most blessed part of a worship service. To "speak grace" is a privilege, a wonder: it is the speaking of a holy mystery. It seems too good to be true. In fact, it is too good not to be true, and the faithful presider knows that each and *every* time she speaks words like "The mercy of the Lord is from everlasting to everlasting," or "as far as the east is from the west, so far does the Lord put our transgressions from us," or "Friends, believe the good news! In Jesus Christ we are forgiven," she speaks life-giving, life-changing gospel.

The presider who speaks gospel, proclaiming forgiveness and calling us forth to new life, must not speak these words without conviction. The declaration of forgiveness is not the pat on the head after the tongue-lashing, or the

"Oh, it's all right," sighed after the punishment has been meted out. It is the announcing of unfathomable love in the face of our flaws and failures—love that receives all, covers all, heals all. That announcement of divine mercy comes riding on the breath of another flawed creature, the presider. The voice that proclaims forgiveness may sometimes falter or crack, but it speaks these words with passion, hope, and joy.

Speaking Blessing

A woman with a scarf over her head hoists her six-year-old up onto the first step of the school bus. "Goodbye," she says.

A father on the phone with his freshman son has just finished bawling him out for his poor grades. There is mostly silence at the other end of the line. "Well, goodbye," the father says.

When the girl at the airport hears the announcement that her plane is starting to board, she turns to the boy who is seeing her off. "I guess this is goodbye," she says.

The noise of the traffic almost drowns out the sound of the word, but the shape of it lingers on the old man's lips. He tries to look vigorous and resourceful as he holds out his hand to the other old man. "Goodbye." This time they say it so nearly in unison that it makes them both smile.

It was a long while ago that the words *God be with you* disappeared into the word *goodbye*, but every now and again some trace of them still glimmers through.[29]

This is how Frederick Buechner describes what happens when we take our leave from one another. "God be with you" is indeed what we want to say, what we need to say, to fill the crevices of fear and doubt, to mend the fissures of the hurts we have caused, to entrust one another to the sure and abiding care of God.

This is why, when we come to the end of the worship service, someone needs to say something more than "G'wan, get outta here!" And so there is a benediction. It seems like a small thing, this ritual good-bye, but as Emily Brink has said, "Benedictions are more than pious wishes."[30] Indeed, this liturgical snippet that is often overlooked, misunderstood, or poorly enacted is a moment of profound theological and pastoral significance, in which God speaks blessing to the people gathered in God's name. Providential care is proclaimed, the people's trust is renewed, and we affirm once again the covenant relationship that springs forth from this holy economy. This benediction, it seems, is not such a small thing after all.

Perhaps the most familiar liturgical blessing is the "Aaronic benediction" found in Numbers 6:

> The Lord bless you and keep you.
> The Lord be kind and gracious to you.
> The Lord look upon you with favor
> and give you peace.[31]

Here the Hebrew people have been rescued from slavery; they make a sanctuary for God's abiding presence and ordain priests to lead them in worship. They gather to pray and then, at the end of their first service of worship, Aaron speaks these words that reflect the relationship between God and God's people. This is more than a felicitously phrased set of good wishes from priest to people; it is Yahweh who gives the blessing. And, for Yahweh, blessing is no vague spiritual thing, but the stuff of abundant life: children, land, health, wealth, flocks, and fruitfulness. Each phrase of the blessing, in fact, reveals another layer of divine favor. This is the God who keeps God's people—indeed, the whole world—providing protection and care, preserving life in the face of all manner of threats and trials. This is a God of kindness, a God of grace, who shows mercy, forgives sins, and saves the people from every evil.[32] Aaron's blessing ends with a prayer for God's peace, God's *shalom*: the end of conflict, physical health, prosperity, safety, contentment. The God who saved the people from death continually blesses them, bestowing on them everything they need to live and thrive and grow.[33] This blessing, then, is an intimate utterance that is at once proclamation, prayer, and promise; it calls to memory God's saving acts, asks God to continue to save and to bless, and claims the covenant relationship that is reflected between the One who blesses and those who are blessed.

It is not always easy to believe that there is a current of grace that runs through life, to affirm that "history is a purposive unfolding rather than 'one damned thing after another.'" Paul Pruyser puts it well: "Belief in providence is belief in order and meaning—ultimately a belief in divine benevolence.... Belief in providence is trust in the divine hands and an awareness of the possibility of having contact with them."[34] That's just the sort of thing that brings us face to face with the absurdity of grace. "What holds us back from trusting God," Carolyn Gratton says, "is that we cannot even imagine the heart of Christianity, the utterly gratuitous love of God that comes to us in Christ."[35] Yet that is precisely what is proclaimed in the benediction that closes our worship each Sunday morning.

This is not to imply that blessing means days full of warmth and comfort food. Flannery O'Connor put it well when she said that "people don't realize how much religion costs. They think faith is a big electric blanket, when of course it is the cross. It is much harder to believe than not to believe."[36] Blessing carries with it not the promise of a trouble-free life, but the pledge of God's active presence among the people who seek to do God's work in the world—even in the face of the worst the world can give. That sense is reflected in these examples of scriptural charge and blessing from Deuteronomy and from 1 Thessalonians:

> Be strong and of good courage; do not fear;
>   for it is God who goes with you,
>   and God will never fail you nor forsake you.
> Go in peace. Amen.[37]

> Go in peace, be very courageous, hold on to what is good,
>   do not return evil for evil, encourage the fainthearted,
> support the weak, help the afflicted, honor all people,
>   love and serve the Lord, rejoicing in the power of the Holy Spirit;
> and the grace of our Lord Jesus Christ be with you.[38]

In the face of challenge, we trust. In the face of tragedy, we trust. In the dark night of the soul, we trust. Even in death, we trust. As Patrick Miller reminds us, "Those who have seen the salvation and blessing of God continue on in the presence and work of Jesus Christ know that the good news given is that divine care does not stop at death. The seal of that is Jesus Christ himself."[39] Walking in the knowledge of such providence changes our whole way of being, as we are transformed into agents of the very blessing we have received.

The benediction, then, is not so much an ending to worship as it is a "sending for worshipful work."[40] We are emboldened and empowered because we go out trusting not in our own strength or commitment or fervor or faith, but in the ongoing, unwavering providence of God. Blessing is not just a nice, comfortable sweater to don before heading out into the chilly world of reality. Blessing is power to live a life of faith and service, freed from the grip of fear and confident of the sustenance of a benevolent God. These nice words with which we close out a service of worship, then, are not so benign as we might have once thought. It matters that they are spoken, and it matters that they are spoken well.

Pronouncing the benediction is usually understood as the prerogative of the minister. This does not mean, of course, that there is anything ontologically superior about the one who is ordained to the ministry of Word and

Sacrament; it does, however, acknowledge that blessing the people "is a basic dimension in the life of ministering to and for the congregation."[41] Furthermore, there is symbolic power in entrusting those tasks to the one the body calls forth and ordains for the purpose of proclaiming the gospel in the spoken and embodied word.

The power of symbol often goes unrecognized in our culture, which has been shaped by Enlightenment thinking. I once took part in a worship service where the offerings for the local food pantry were brought forth in a basket so large it had to be carried by two people, one on each side. Wow! I thought, now that really speaks of the generosity of God and of the spirit of giving enacted in this congregation! Upon returning home, I described the scene to a friend, comparing it to the small breadbasket offering in our own church, which held only a can or two and a box of macaroni. "Oh, well," she replied, "it's only a symbol."

Ah, but it is not "only a symbol." Don Saliers is one author who has written eloquently about how symbolic languages work. "As with poetry and literature," he explains, "the symbols in living liturgy mean more than they say, and they present to human beings much more than what appears."[42] Flannery O'Connor was even more to the point. Confronted with a friend's remark that the Eucharist was, for her, a symbol, Flannery O'Connor replied, "Well, if it's a symbol, to hell with it."[43]

Indeed, worship is full of symbols, and the presider is one of them. Like bread broken, wine poured, and water splashed, the very person of the pastor is a symbol, communicating the presence of the Word of God in the midst of the people. That this person is the one who blesses represents, beyond what our words can say, that the benediction spoken comes not only from the pastor but also from God's own heart.

This makes the benediction one of the most profound pastoral acts of all. It is, all at once, proclamation, prayer, and promise. It is an expression of relationships that are forged simultaneously: love and care of pastor for people; trust and covenant between the people and God; love between members of the body; and the "worshipful work" that is the expression of love of Christ's church for the whole world. This is no perfunctory act at all, this blessing. It is at the heart of our life as Christians together.

Pruyser, writing from his perspective as a psychologist interested in pastoral care, makes an astute observation about the way ministers carry out this important act of blessing.

When worship leaders perform sloppily in their liturgical work, they are obviously not attributing a high professional value to this part of their activities. And when they perform badly in benedictions, the unspoken messages to the congregation are that: (1) benedictions are rather meaningless, (2) the pastor does not deem the people worthy of receiving them, (3) the pastor himself has long given up thoughts of providence, or (4) the pastor refuses to shoulder the shepherd's role. Perhaps more important than all these conjectures is that he does not seem to know enough about people and their needs or that he is so caught up in his own conflicts that he cannot respond to the needs of others. Although these deeper problems cannot be solved by attempting to give the liturgical benediction properly, movements and gestures are psychodynamically so important in life and are so closely interwoven with emotion that attempts at performing the proper motion are very likely to stimulate the corresponding emotion also. Giving the benediction is not only a meaningful act but like most liturgical words and motions also a beautiful act, and its proper aesthetic performance may give several side benefits to the pastor as well as convey a great gift to the congregation.[44]

What is clear from Pruyser's discussion is that it is impossible to separate the personal from the pastoral. Without a deep conviction about the providence of God, one cannot bless. If one assumes that the words of the benediction are devoid of any divine element, then it becomes little more than what Pruyser calls "pastoral niceness."[45] If one imagines that the benediction is merely a time to assume a posture of ecclesial authority, the words of blessing do not ring true. But if one looks into the eyes of those beloved who are called children of God, aching with love for them in all of their quirks and faults and wonderful giftedness, extending arms in a gesture not unlike the laying on of hands, and speaks a benediction—well, then, it is a thing of deep and holy beauty.

In Marilynne Robinson's acclaimed novel *Gilead* is the story of the Rev. John Ames, an aging minister. Near the end of the story, his best friend, Boughton, is dying. Boughton's son (and John Ames's namesake) was a young man who brought his father nothing but trouble and heartache. He made all the wrong choices and now, true to form, was leaving town—and leaving his dying father to depart this world alone. The young man had a bond with the old minister, though, and on the day he sneaked out of town the Rev. Ames met him. After a few halting attempts at conversation, the elder man tells the younger that if he'd accept a few dollars from him, it would be a kindness. He laughed and said he thought he could do that. They sat for a moment, and then the minister spoke:

> "The thing I would like, actually, is to bless you."
> He shrugged. "What would that involve?"

"Well, as I envisage it, it would involve my placing my hand on your brow and asking the protection of God for you. But if it would be embarrassing—" There were a few people on the street.

"No, no," he said, "that doesn't matter." And he took his hat off and set it on his knee and closed his eyes and lowered his head, almost rested it against my hand, and I did bless him to the limit of my powers, whatever they are, repeating the benediction from Numbers, of course—"The Lord make his face to shine upon thee, and be gracious unto thee: The Lord lift up his countenance upon thee, and give thee peace." Nothing could be more beautiful than that, or more expressive of my feelings, certainly, or more sufficient, for that matter. Then, when he didn't open his eyes or lift up his head, I said, "Lord, bless John Ames Boughton, this beloved son and brother and husband and father." Then he sat back and looked at me as if he were waking out of a dream.[46]

Sometimes a blessing is all we have to give—but it is a mighty thing to give. In the seemingly simple act of blessing, we do nothing less than proclaim God's providence, pray God's immanence, and claim the promise of God's live-giving movement throughout the whole world and in our own small lives.

The Sacramentality of Speech: Liturgy

We have explored the implications of the sacramentality of speech for proclamation; there are still other implications for liturgy and the language of prayer. If our bodies bear forth the word of God, they also bear forth the people's prayers. For the God who speaks is also the God who listens, and the words we speak to God's people, and with God's people, are also sacred. To put it simply, again, our words matter. In worship there are no throwaway lines.

In an effort to be hospitable (and, to be honest, likable), presiders can fall into the trap of mistaking a familiar, intimate, easygoing manner with good worship leadership. Often that means sloppy speech—that is, inattentiveness to the way language works and an overdependence on charisma and personal style. The result is that worship leadership becomes more about the presider's ability to be winsome or persuasive—even emotionally manipulative—rather than about gathering with the rest of the body in the presence of God. For example, some pastors begin a worship service by exclaiming, with a big smile, "Good morning! It's good to see you here!" thus communicating that the pastor, not God, is the one to be pleased. Once I heard a minister begin the service by saying, "Well, at least the Falcons won last week," as though we'd all gathered for the pregame show rather than the worship of the holy God.

This is not to argue for grim, tight-lipped presiding, or to advocate formality over informality. It is, however, to insist that the language used in worship ought to be biblical, creative, eloquent, imaginative, and expansive—language that says that something is happening here that happens nowhere else, language that invites us into an event, a way of being, and the expectation that we will encounter the holy. Worship may be like the theater, but worshipers are participants, not audience. It may be like a community meeting, but worshipers come not only to meet one another but also to meet the holy God. It may be a place where we come to learn doctrine, or to grow spiritually, but more than anything it is a place we come to hear the voice of God and to raise our hearts and hands and voices in return. It may be a place where we are summoned to acts of justice and love, but we do not come to hear our politics confirmed. Worship is more than all this, and our language must be strong enough, and beautiful enough, to bear it. As Richard Lischer puts it, "The profound questions of meaning cannot be answered by an ordered series of talking points. To do so is to falsify and cheapen divine revelation."[47] Catherine Madsen puts it just as insistently: "Something far more important than intellectual assent is at stake in liturgy. It is the integration of the body and the personality into the community, of each person's full energies into the community's work."[48] And again, "Theologians and scholars of religion have studied the doctrines, the development, the anthropology, the sociology and the politics of liturgy—everything but the moment when our souls ring in sympathy with a phrase and want to obey it. But that moment of resonance is what distinguishes prayer (and some poetry) from all other speech."[49] In other words, there is a poetic dimension to the language of worship that cannot be ignored.

It is time to attend more carefully to the words we speak, to take into account what T. S. Eliot called the "auditory imagination": "the feeling for syllable and rhythm, penetrating far below the conscious levels of thought and feeling, invigorating every word; sinking to the most primitive and forgotten, returning to an origin and bringing something back, . . . fusing the most ancient and civilized mentalities."[50] In other words, we begin by realizing that speaking is not only about explaining, and hearing is not simply about understanding; they are also about apprehending, even experiencing, words, the Word. Or, even better, it is about being grasped by the Word, taken hold of, taken over.

Few have expressed this as persuasively as Gail Ramshaw, who in describing the poetic nature of liturgical language argues that "the vocabulary and the grammar of worship have at their root the multivalence and ambiguity with which our age seems uneasy."[51]

> Not only the language, but also the symbols of our liturgical experience are metaphors. We call the water of baptism, whether three drops or a bathful, a flood that drowns and a fountain that washes. It is both a womb of birth and the tomb of death. There is in our use of water in baptism the poem's inconsistency, rather than the logical extension found in discursive philosophy. We believe that baptism drowns, like Noah's flood and the Red Sea; yet in these stories God's people, far from drowning by water, escape the wet grave. So also with the meal. This bread and wine is the Last Supper, the meal at Emmaus, the body of Christ, the eschatological banquet, the food shared with Moses and the elders on the mountain of God. We are the body of Christ, sharing in the body of Christ, sharing the body of Christ. It is hardly surprising that our theological explanations of the sacraments are inadequate to the metaphors of the liturgical experience. The community of faith demonstrates through its liturgical life its participation in a reality too complex for discursive description.[52]

The language of liturgy, when understood as more poetic than discursive, opens up possibilities for ongoing revelation. There are traditions that have labored long and well to revise their liturgies so that the language is evocative, deep, and lively, and others who have tried valiantly with less success.

The fact is, it is hard work. Kathleen Norris relays the story of how she once enlisted poets Denise Levertov and Richard Wilbur to help her review the work of a liturgy committee. "One day I received a letter from a woman on the translation committee, a brilliant biblical scholar, who wrote of the new translations: 'We think they're pretty good poems.' Also in the mail was a note from Levertov, who said, 'It's all there except the poetry.'"[53] Consider this example: One could imagine opening an order of worship and encountering a prayer of confession something like this:

> God of mercy, sometimes we do things we don't mean to do, and other times we don't do the things we should. We don't love you and we don't love each other very well, either. Forgive our mistakes and help us to do better in the future because we want to be the best people we can be.

This prayer is adequate theologically (for the most part), and it's understandable. No one would say this prayer sings, though; the language lumbers along in such a simple and colloquial fashion that one suspects that God isn't all that special. Consider now the same prayer, wrought in rhythmic language that echoes Scripture and reflects a more theologically nuanced understanding of the human condition and our relationship to God:

Merciful God,
we confess that we have sinned against you
in thought, word, and deed,
by what we have done,
and by what we have left undone.
We have not loved you
with our whole heart and mind and strength.
We have not loved our neighbors as ourselves.

In your mercy forgive what we have been,
help us amend what we are,
and direct what we shall be,
so that we may delight in your will
and walk in your ways,
to the glory of your holy name.[54]

This language is not poetry, but it speaks in poetic language—language that we dare to speak to the creator of the cosmos, words that are imaginative and graceful without being pompous or overwrought.

To advocate prayer language with poetic sensibilities is not necessarily to insist that all prayers be written. In Reformed churches, and in some "free" churches as well, there is a fluid movement between form and freedom when it comes to speech and act in worship. Those who preside in traditions without a prayer book, those who find themselves creatively adapting their church's prescribed liturgy, or those who consistently write liturgical texts for their congregations will find their prayers will better bear the weight of the gospel if they attend to the marks of good liturgical language.

Some Marks of Effective Liturgical Language

As with most of life, liturgical language is all about balance. Good liturgical language is not so formal and stiff that it is distancing, nor is it so casual that it sounds overly familiar and slangy. Annie Dillard was on to something when she defined liturgy as "certain words which people have successfully addressed to God without their getting killed."[55] What does this language sound like? It has rhythm and tone, beauty of expression and economy of words, whether it is planned or extemporaneous.

Gail Ramshaw wisely advises would-be liturgists to know the difference between "colloquial" and "vernacular" speech.[56] On the one hand, liturgical language needs to be language that we understand. At the same time, however, the church needs language that bears the weight of the gospel, words that express not only intimacy, but also awe and humility, as we dare to address the creator of the cosmos. Sometimes we miss the mark. In her essay "Drawing on Metaphor," Kathleen Norris quotes a prime example: "Use this hour to get our perspectives straight,"[57] one prayer of confession dully rang out in a service she attended, as if the worshipers were giving instructions on how to give them a spiritual tune-up in sixty minutes or less. Is this really the sort of thing we want to say to God? The Evangelical Lutheran Church's reflections on language that appear in *Principles for Worship* state it well: "The language of worship is both ordinary and extraordinary. . . . It uses carefully crafted vernacular speech as well as words and expressions not common in everyday speech," such as vocabulary drawn from the Bible and from tradition that Christians share.[58]

This balance between ordinary and extraordinary is difficult to achieve when crafting liturgical language. Over the last half century, churches have strived to imbue their worship with language that speaks to the people of their time. In Gilbert Ostdiek's chronicling of the work of the International Commission on English in the Liturgy (ICEL), we can see a bit of the evolution of style in the Roman Church's prayer language over the course of the twentieth century. He compares three versions of the opening prayer for the Ninth Sunday in Ordinary Time from the Roman Sacramentary, composed in different decades.

1941

O God, whose Providence never fails in its plans, we humbly plead for ourselves that Thou remove whatever may be harmful and grant whatever may be useful. Through our Lord . . .

1973

Father, your love never fails.
Hear our call.
Keep us from danger
and provide for all our needs.
Grant this . . .

1995

O God,
You order the course of our lives
With unfailing providence.
Remove from our path whatever is harmful
and grant us those things that work to our good.
We ask this . . .

Ostdiek explains that in the first version one can hear the sort of formal language that, at the time, was thought to convey a sense of holiness and awe. By the 1970s, however, liturgists were striving to strip away all pretense and created texts that were accessible and even minimalist. The language was more direct and intimate, to be sure, but it was also choppy and abrupt. Gone was any sense of poetic imagination, and the speech was too colloquial. The 1995 text shows the linguistic pendulum swinging back toward fuller, more heightened language. While it is still immediate and intelligible, there is a balance between grace and gravity here. While such a prayer text might be adjusted for use in different contexts, the latter text shows a depth of theological understanding as well as a richness of language that serves the church well.[59]

Employing poetic language, then, does not necessarily mean that liturgy cannot make use of straightforward vocabulary and grammatical structure. One way of doing this is to avoid unfamiliar and multisyllabic words that cause people to stumble, or overly long sentences that cloud meaning. Norris points to the following example of language that does just the opposite in a prayer of confession: "We are easy prey, living God, to slick advertising, and, as a result, / We always fall victim to our own acquisitiveness and that of our society and culture."[60] This language is convoluted: "acquisitiveness" is something of a tongue twister, and the sentence structure makes it difficult to apprehend quickly the meaning of the words. Furthermore, this sentence points to another pitfall in modern liturgical speech. More than one presider has depended on the parlance of popular psychology without even realizing it. Norris provides another irresistible example: "We pray, Father, for the One Person Family Unit that they will know that you are their partner in life."[61] Not only is that sentence awkward, but it also relies on a particular sociological framework. There is a place for therapeutic concerns in the church, but as a worshiping people the primary lenses through which we view the world—and therefore the primary speech we use to speak of, and to, God— is biblical and theological. Better, then, to pray "Loving God, / our source and our strength, / draw near all those who live alone / and be their companion along the way." Speaking language drawn from Scripture and from the church's tradition, even while employing new images and metaphors, tethers us to the holy and reminds us that there is a wisdom and love that transcends all earthly language. Norris calls this "incarnational language"—it does not hold us at a distance, but conveys that something real and holy and profound is happening here. A prayer such as this one from ICEL uses this sort of language well:

O God,
whose word burns like a fire within us,
grant us a bold and faithful spirit,
that in your strength we may be unafraid
to speak your word
and follow where you lead.[62]

The language is straightforward without being slangy, poetic without being overwrought, with evocative images and an internal rhythm that allows it to be spoken aloud with ease.

Finding One's Voice

Speaking is a physical act that relies on breath; speech, like song, rides on the air. And in order to have breath, one must have strength and flexibility. As singers and actors know, producing sound requires one's whole body. The voice emerges not simply from the lips or the mouth or even the throat, but also from the bottom of the feet. Strong and flexible legs and an elastic, firm, and expansive core anchor the sound. Free shoulders and a loose neck allow the sound to float freely, and an open, rounded mouth with lips to shape pure vowels produces a sound that is buoyant, vibrant, and expressive.

Those with little experience in vocal production might try a couple of simple exercises that illustrate the point. First, stand up, raise one finger and hold it a few inches in front of your mouth, and place your other hand on your midsection. Pretending that your finger is a candle, practice blowing out the flame in a series of short puffs. You'll feel your core expand and contract quickly as you take in and expel air. Next, practice yawning, feeling the soft palate rise into an arc. Holding the feeling of a yawn, make a sound like a siren, imagining the sound bouncing off the highest point of the roof of your mouth. You will feel your whole body engaged as you stand firmly on both feet, expand your core to inhale, firm up your middle as you make sound, and feel your head resonate as your voice emerges.[63]

The voice, then, comes from the whole body and also from the soul, for the voice carries not only sound, but also emotion. Figuring out the physical nature of sound production is only one step; the rest of the work is spiritual. Siobhán Garrigan tells about her own attempts to figure out how she should sound when leading worship, and how she finally realized that "you have to find your power in your real voice: the voice that can bear the word of God; the voice whose accent you cannot fake." She continues:

> The spirituality of presiding is, I think, all in your voice. Your tone, words, cadence, timing, timbre, your sounds, your voice's pauses and silences—all conspire to make your voice the most versatile and powerful tool you have to lead others. Be loud and hectoring and you'll scare. Be soft and supple and you'll entice. Use too many clever words and you'll block. Use too much "preacher voice" and they won't believe you. No jazz at all and the words fall flat. You proclaim, invite, dedicate, pray, teach, sing, lead, chant, dream, lament, challenge, cry—and all with your voice. . . . What's in your voice is your presence. And what's in your presence as you preside can be God's spirit or not.[64]

Siobhán Garrigan does, in fact, have an exquisite speaking voice, and she uses it well. One does hear presence in her voice, and when she presides, people often say that they feel they have been led into prayer. Not long after she wrote these words, however, her doctor found a small lump beside her uvula, and for two and a half months she did not know whether she would be able to speak or sing. Thankfully, the lump was found to be benign, but the experience made her rethink her earlier convictions. She came to the point of "pondering less the voice-bit and more the presence-bit."[65]

Garrigan's experience offered a good corrective to her theology and spirituality of presiding. I remember participating in a worship conference where one of the leaders spoke in a high, quiet, raspy voice. An attendee, thinking the leader was ailing, promised to pray for his recovery. "Oh, my voice has been like this for years," the leader explained. "Well, I'll still pray for you," the sincere but misguided attendee responded. "God still does miracles." In fact, God had been working miracles through this leader and his raspy voice for a long time. As Garrigan found out, presence—and the faithful leading that goes with it—is more important than expressiveness or beauty.

The faithful and effective presider must continually delve into the deep wells of faith. She must pray without ceasing. In spite of questions and in the face of frailty and infirmity she must carry on, shouldering the responsibility of being the community's "sayer of grace." Some weeks are easier than others. Sometimes weariness overtakes us. Sometimes a dryness pervades the soul for a long time. Sometimes emotions well up without notice, causing the voice to waver or crack, showing something of ourselves that we thought was safely hidden. It is said that the eyes are the window to the soul; the voice is its sounding board. This is, perhaps, what makes presiding such a vulnerable thing. For these words—carrying this Word—are sounded by the voice, which rides on the very breath of our fragile bodies and souls

And yet the voice is, at the same time, a remarkable tool. For it is the voice, perhaps even more than the body's gestures or movements, that expresses the passion of life with God—all the lament and all the praise, all the wonder and anger and doubt, all the joy and awe. God's Word is a living word, and it is the human voice that causes gospel words to resonate through the body of Christ, and out into the world.

One thing needs yet to be said. Whether the presider is proclaiming gospel or leading in prayer, she must believe what she says. To paraphrase Paul, though I may speak with the tongues of angels yet believe not a word of it, I am but a noisy clanging of cymbals. Even the most faithful of presiders lives with questions and doubt; it is part of the life of faith to do so. There may even be days when conviction is expressed more out of obedience than from strength of feeling. And yet, the blessed burden remains: one who leads in worship must do so from a place of deep faith. Whether reading or speaking memorized texts, or praying extemporaneously, the Word and the words must be breathed in, lived with, even dwelt in, and breathed out again, vibrating with sound and Spirit.

For Further Reading

Ronald P. Byars. *What Language Shall I Borrow? The Bible and Christian Worship.* Grand Rapids: Wm. B. Eerdmans Publishing Co., 2008.

Ruth Duck. *Finding Words for Worship.* Louisville, KY: Westminster/John Knox Press, 1995.

Gail Ramshaw. *Reviving Sacred Speech: The Meaning of Liturgical Language, Second Thoughts on Christ in Sacred Speech.* Akron: OSL Publications, 2000.

Laurence Hull Stookey. *Let the Whole Church Say, Amen!* Nashville: Abingdon Press, 2001.

Chapter 5

The Hands

Gesture and Touch

When my grown sons were young boys, we took a lot of car trips. On one particularly long journey, after we had exhausted the usual repertoire of the license-plate hunt and Twenty Questions, they came up with a game of their own. They took pieces of drawing paper and made two signs. One said, "Hello!" That one went in the front passenger window. The second said "How is your day going?" That one was held up in the back passenger window. It then became my job to pass as many cars as possible.

We were surprised, then delighted, at how many people responded to the signs. The driver of nearly every car we passed gave us an honest answer, using the only method of communication available: his or her hands. We got some thumbs-up signals, some fingers circled in an OK sign, a few thumbs down, and quite a number of hands wavering back and forth in a so-so pattern. It was great entertainment—and a reminder of how a simple gesture between people can communicate.

An even more compelling account of the power of gesture comes from a now-prominent U.S. Senator who was held and tortured in a POW camp in Vietnam. One night his captors bound him with excruciatingly tight ropes and left him in a cold, dark room to suffer alone through the night. Not long after they departed, one of the guards came back into the room. He did not speak, but loosened the ropes and left. Just before daybreak, he slipped into the room and retightened the ropes before his comrades returned.

Soon thereafter Christmas morning dawned on the camp, and the prisoner stood alone in a dusty courtyard. The same guard walked up and stood next to him. Again, he did not speak. After a few moments he took his sandal and scratched a cross in the dirt. The two of them stood side by side, silently venerating the symbol. Then the guard scuffed out the marks and left.[1] Such a gesture can be a powerful thing, especially when there is a great deal at stake.

Whenever God's people gather for worship, there *is* a great deal at stake. Every Sunday is not a matter of life and death for every person, but our cumulative experience means that what happens in worship can mean the difference between hope and despair for some of us on any given day, and eventually for us all. That means that even something as seemingly simple as a gesture or a touch can bear great meaning.

Anyone who has ever sung or played under the direction of a good conductor, or even watched one at work, knows that hands are a powerful tool of communication. A hand held up in gentle persuasion evokes a softly plaintive tone; an arm jabbing the air urges the musicians on to a forceful, punctuated sound; hands suspended and barely moving keep the notes spinning as though they might never end. A gesture, well conceived and well wrought, is a powerful thing.

Worship is full of such gestures, even though we may not stop to think about it as such. The passing of the peace of Christ, the laying on of hands, the breaking of bread, even an invitation to stand—all involve some sort of bodily gesture. Many presiders, however, give little thought to the power of gesture. Some of us gesticulate wildly in conversation but freeze into rigid caution when leading worship. Some of us are naturally reserved and simply do not move around very much. Others of us flail indiscriminately so that our gestures are actually sources of distraction rather than communication. The effective presider, however, is intentional about gestures, using them in ways that free us from using too many words or that enhance the meaning of the words we do speak. Romano Guardini once said that "God has given us our hands in order that we may 'carry our souls' in them."[2] Indeed, the hands are remarkable tools—beautiful, eloquent, and expressive—and key to effective presiding.

Gestures in Worship

Most presiders have a sense that they ought to be doing something besides simply standing up front and talking, but many of us have trouble imagining what that may be. Except for the hyperactive among us, who tend to be in constant (though unthinking) motion, worship leaders often fall into one of two traps: gesturing only rarely (say, only at the benediction) or thrusting the arms out in a generic arms-open posture, which can convey warmth and welcome, but when used for every element of a service ceases to bear meaning.

The wise worship leader will cultivate a repertoire of gestures for the various tasks of presiding. The key to gestures that convey meaning is simple:

think about the words that are being said. If, for instance, you are calling people to worship, you might extend your arms outward toward the people. If you are calling them to confession, however, you might simply stand with your arms at your sides, or with your hands loosely joined or touching in front of you, in a posture of humility. After declaring the forgiveness of God, an "Alleluia!" or "Thanks be to God!" might cause the presider's hands to rise up in an embodied expression of praise. The key is to be intentional with gestures, so that they are not used indiscriminately, or simply tacked on to the words being spoken. Effective gestures are organic extensions of the words being spoken.

A common posture for prayer is called by some the *orans* (literally, "the one who prays"), or orant position. The presider stands with arms extended outward and palms turned upward in a gesture that can be traced back to early renderings of Christians at prayer.[3] If this is an unfamiliar stance, try it out: with elbows near (but not touching) the torso, extend your arms to each side, hands upturned. Once you become used to this position, it seems a natural way to pray—the very posture of your body says that you are lifting prayers to God, voicing them humbly on behalf of all who are present. It is "a stance of openness and vulnerability to God, as well as a gesture of reaching toward God."[4] If this gesture is used only for prayer, then the whole assembly grasps the meaning of it: it is not for addressing the congregation or proclaiming a text, but for speaking to God.

Gestures are not always tied to spoken words; some gestures can actually take the place of speech. Simple cues to stand (one or both hands open before you in a rising motion) or to sit (hands open in the same way, but moving in a lowering motion) can reduce the amount of unnecessary chatter in a worship service. Consider, for instance, two scenarios. In one, the presider stands and says, "I invite you now to please stand and together we will pray the litany of intercession, which you will find printed in your bulletin." In another, the presider simply stands and raises an open hand or hands to indicate to the congregation that they, too, may stand. If all are following a printed liturgy, prayer book, or projected words, the presider then simply says, "Let us pray," and the congregation knows to take part. While the first scenario is not "wrong," a service can get weighed down by words when sets of instructions accompany every move.

There are some who argue that spoken instructions are more hospitable, because they provide explanations for newcomers. I contend, however, that newcomers are drawn not so much to clarity as to the sense that people are intently engaged in worship. Craig Satterlee expresses a similar view when he asserts: "Like all human rituals, newcomers cannot fully, completely, and instantly participate. The most profound impression that worship may make on a stranger is that an assembly of believing and doubting Christians is honestly engaged with God."[5] When the congregation as a body follows a simple gesture of the presider, the newcomer experiences a sense of unity of purpose and practice. If this sense of oneness is combined with genuine warmth and welcome from both congregation and worship leaders, then newcomers are drawn to something of which they too would like to be a part.

Even when introducing a new practice, sometimes gesture is often all one needs. Imagine that you are inviting people to join in intercessory prayers that involve a congregational response. You could, of course, explain what is about to happen: "I invite you to join me now in prayer. As I offer petitions for the world and the church, I will say, 'God of mercy,' to which you will reply, 'Hear our prayer.'" That is an acceptable way to instruct people as to the form the prayer will take, but again, it is word-heavy. It is actually possible to give such instructions by use of a simple gesture. Consider this introduction instead: "Let us pray together, saying, 'God of mercy' [your hands are placed on your chest], 'hear our prayer' [your hands are extended to the people, indicating that this is their spoken part]. 'God of mercy' [hands back on your chest], 'hear our prayer' [hands extended to the congregation once again]." With the repetition of those words and simple gestures, congregations understand immediately that we are entering into a responsive form of prayer. Once a congregation catches on to the idea that the presider will be giving visual cues rather than long sets of verbal instructions, the people become more attentive, expecting that they will be led visually as well as aurally. Furthermore, the words spoken in prayer are not buried under an avalanche of explanation.[6]

All of this can sound terribly scripted, especially to those who lead worship in a freer, more extemporaneous style. In fact, communicating through gestures, when those gestures are enacted thoughtfully and intentionally, can seem quite natural when the presider is well prepared and has thought through the rhythm and sequence of the service. As we have already seen, knowing the pattern of worship by heart, and understanding the deep logic of each element of that pattern, enables the presider to lead with confidence and humility. The task of presiding is not so much about performing the proper gestures at the proper times and with the proper finesse, as about enabling the worship of the people and making space for God to meet us there.

If we were to resist the notion that the gestures of the presider are of any import, or presume that a motionless leader is good enough, Mark Searle's reflection on bowing might well bring us to understanding what is at stake:

"Zedekiah was one and twenty years old when he began to reign. . . . And he did that which was evil in the sight of the Lord his God, and humbled not himself before Jeremiah the prophet speaking from the mouth of the Lord . . . but he stiffened his neck and hardened his heart from turning unto the Lord God of Israel."

Unbending, unyielding,
unacknowledging God or man.

Without a supple neck
how could I greet my neighbor in a crowd?
how could I tell my child she is doing well?
how could I express my grief and shame?
how could I assent without interrupting?
how could I show sadness in the face of suffering?
how could I show solidarity with one who speaks?
how could I offer my silent respect to a great lady?
how could I honor an eminent man?
how could I accept the verdict of my peers?
. . . simply, silently, wordlessly?

how could I surrender to the blessing
of the One who alone can deliver me out of death?

how could I acknowledge
that there is only one Name
by which I can be saved—
the name of Jesus?[7]

Our gestures and posture are important in our daily encounters with one another, mirroring our ability to stand with vulnerability and humility before the God of grace. No less important are they in the work of leading worship, to which we are called.

Gesture at the Eucharistic Table

It is especially appropriate to think of the embodied nature of worship when considering presiding at the Lord's Table, where we are immersed in layers of language about the body. We hear it in the account of Jesus' taking bread, blessing it, breaking it, and giving it to his disciples, and in Jesus' assertion that the bread he gives is his own body. In presiding at the Table, then, it is natural for us to use not just our voices but also our own bodies, especially our hands—not only in the taking, the blessing, the breaking, and the giving, but also in the praying of the eucharistic prayer.

Gestures at the table are intentional, yet organic to the action; in other words, they are not so much prescribed as they are expressive of what is happening. For example, when the presider says to the people, "The Lord be with you," it is natural to extend the arms toward the people, hands open and outstretched, palms upward, in a gesture of invitation. In turn, the people might extend a hand toward the presider as they reply, "And also with you," in a sharing of that affirmation that Christ is indeed in our midst. Likewise, the presider who embodies the words "Lift up your hearts" might quite naturally lift the hands upward (and so might some brave folks in the congregation!). When speaking, "Let us give thanks to the Lord our God," it seems natural to bring the hands downward and in front of the body, clasped or pressed together in a gesture of thankful prayer. This series of movements need not be done with military precision, but rather as simple, flowing, and connected expressions of the words being spoken.

In the early days of my ministry, I was grateful to have a book to clutch as I stood trembling at the Lord's Table. In more recent years, however, fear has given way to joy as I have lived into the gorgeous logic of classic, Trinitarian, eucharistic prayer. What a remarkable, awesome, joyful story we get to tell when we remember before God all the amazing things God has done for the people—creating a wondrous world, making a covenant with us, delivering us from bondage to freedom, living in our flesh as Jesus Christ to feed and teach and heal, and even sharing in our dying that we might share in his rising. It is as if we are recalling our favorite stories with a beloved spouse or parent or child: Remember when you got me out of that scrape. . . . Remember when you first told me you loved me. . . . Remember when you kissed my cuts to make them better. . . . Remember when . . . Each story reminds us of God's faithfulness in the past, God's promises for the future, God's continuing presence with us now—and why we are so filled with love and gratitude for it all. In lifting this prayer to God, we embody thanksgiving as we extend our arms outward and upward, palms open to heaven. This posture, inherited from early Christians (the *orans,* or orant, position, noted above), gathers the prayers of the whole congregation, presents the gifts of grace on the table, and opens us to communion with Christ.

The next part of the eucharistic prayer, the epiclesis, is where we ask for the pouring out of the Holy Spirit on the bread and wine, and on the people. Presiders might continue in the *orans* position for this, or they might touch the bread and the cup. Or, they might simply allow their hands to move over the people and the elements, not because some magic is passing through their fingers, but as a way of enacting what the words say— participating, if you will, with the Spirit's action. Again, these gestures need not be forced or precise, nor should they be performed with an officious air, but they can flow as a natural outgrowth of the words being spoken. The presider can then move gracefully back into the *orans* position for the concluding Trinitarian doxology.

At this point one might ask why the presider should gesture at all if everyone is praying with head bowed and eyes closed. In fact, eucharistic prayer is a time when people may very well pray with eyes wide open. Although we are, indeed, praying with words, at the heart of it all we are participating in a ritual act. Like baptism, the Lord's Supper is something we *do* and not, primarily, something we *say*. As Calvin explained, Christ's union with us is a mystery so incomprehensible that in this act God shows it to us "in visible signs best adapted to our small capacity."[8] It is, then, utterly appropriate that presider and people alike would pray this prayer while looking at each other and the elements. And if presider (and people) adopt a position of prayer with arms outstretched and hands lifted toward heaven, the dual nature of the Great Thanksgiving as both proclamation and prayer is well expressed.

Once all the words are spoken, it is time to break the bread and pour the wine and share the good gifts of God with God's people. It is nothing less than a mystery that we enact. For in this simple meal is a vast universe of meaning, far more profound than we will ever grasp on this side of heaven. We can never explain it; all we can do, really, is act it out. And so we take the bread with humility and confidence and care, and we tear it. It should take some effort, this tearing of bread, for it is a body being broken. No neatly sliced loaf can convey it so well. And when the bread is broken, it is held up for all to see before it is set down again. Look at those gathered while holding the bread aloft, for these are holy things for holy people. Then the wine is poured, the liquid visible to all, so that the people might see the blood that is shed for them. It can take a little time. It can happen in silence. Finally, the gifts of bread and wine are lifted toward the people, as Christ himself offers them the bread of life and the cup of salvation.

Of course, there is no one prescribed way of doing all this. As Calvin put it nearly five centuries ago, "As for the outward ceremony of the action, . . . these things are indifferent, and left at the church's discretion."[9] What is important, however, is that we give thanks, that the bread is broken and the wine is poured, and that the people eat and drink—to remember all that God has done in Jesus Christ through the power of the Holy Spirit, to anticipate the joy we shall all share at that great heavenly banquet, and to claim the promises of God in the here and now. The tone may be different, depending on whether it is Lent or Easter or All Saints' Day, or what is happening in the world or in the life of the congregation. In all cases, however, the eucharistic prayer is something that presider and congregation do together. The presider tells the well-known story, and the people respond with acclamations of praise ("Holy, holy, holy!") or confidence ("Christ has died, Christ is risen, Christ will come again!"), in a dialogue of thanksgiving before God.

Gestures in the Baptismal Rite

One of the most awe-inspiring privileges of serving as a minister of Word and Sacrament is baptizing. Pastors of denominations who follow a baptismal rite from a worship book must make decisions all along the way about where people should stand, who participates, and so forth. When it comes to the actual baptizing, however, I have two words of advice: one, pray as if you really mean it; and two, use the water visibly, audibly, and generously.

In the wake of years of ecumenical convergence around common prayer, we find that many denominations pray a prayer of thanksgiving over the water. Like the eucharistic prayer, this prayer is a remembering before God: we recall how God gave and sustained life through water, how God delivered God's people through water, how God baptized Jesus Christ in water, opening the way for us to share in his baptism. Finally, we pray for the outpouring of the Spirit in and through the water, that the one being baptized might be raised to new life, joined to Christ, and empowered with the Holy Spirit. This is a story we know well; we remember Noah, the escape from Egypt, and Jesus' baptism. Yet we do not rattle through it as quickly as possible, just to get to the good part. This is the kind of story we tell over and over again at the joyful occasion of welcoming another to the fold—we recite the family history, as it were, as we add one more to our number. This is a story to tell with joy!

Whether baptizing in a font or a baptistry, the presider can make the water visible and audible for the congregation, heightening its communicative power. Water may be poured into the font at the beginning of the baptismal rite, quickly enough to make a splashing sound but slowly enough so that the sound lasts for a while. The presider need not be the one to do this—any member of the congregation, including a child, can pour the water. During the prayer of thanksgiving over the water, the presider may lift the water and let it fall, so the sound of it accompanies the words of the prayer. You might do this once, at the time of the epiclesis ("Send your Spirit to move over this water that it may be a fountain of deliverance and rebirth . . ."), [10] or repeatedly throughout the prayer. Let it be seen, let it be heard—with joy, yes, but always with reverence for the way God gives us birth through water and Spirit.

When it comes to baptizing, there are more decisions to be made. If it is an infant or young child, will she be held over the font and water poured over her head, or will the pastor lower her into the water and submerge her, or will he hold her upright and bring the water to her? If it is an older child, or a teenager, or an adult, will the one being baptized stand with his head over the font so that water might be poured, or will the minister bring water to his head with her own hand? If the baptism takes place in a congregation fortunate to have a large pool for baptizing, it must be decided whether one is baptized by water being poured over the head or if he or she is submerged beneath the water. In any case, let the water be seen and heard. God's grace is abundant to overflowing; if we have water enough to spare, the symbol of that grace should be overflowing as well.

I have a set of photographs given to me by a former parishioner, taken at the baptism of his daughter. In the first picture, the parents, an elder, and I are all gathered around the font. In the second photograph, the elder is a foot or so farther away from me. In the third picture, he has retreated some six or seven feet away; apparently the waters of baptism were so abundant that he was getting doused almost as thoroughly as the child! Everyone in that congregation could see water flying and dripping as little Hannah was baptized in the name of the Father, Son, and Holy Spirit. The amount of water used can be a rich symbol, but it need not be a stumbling block; God is not limited by how little or how much water we use! More important is that the rite be performed with love and a sense of joyful awe at what God is doing.

A word of caution is necessary, however. In some North American churches where infant baptism is practiced, the rite has become domesticated, diminished into what a teacher of mine used to call a "ceremony of cuteness." When infants are baptized, we love to wiggle their toes and pinch their cheeks and "ooh" and "aah." Of course, there is nothing wrong with cooing at a baby. Yet we dare not miss the significance of what is happening in this remarkable rite. This adorable child is being snatched from the jaws of death. In baptism we proclaim that this one is being claimed by God: "Neither death, nor life, nor angels, nor rulers, nor things present, nor things to come, nor powers, nor height, nor depth, nor anything else in all creation," will separate this one from the love of God in Jesus Christ our Lord (Rom. 8:38–39). Perhaps we should be raising this child above our heads, still dripping from the font, proclaiming that she has been rescued from all that can harm her. And then, after we wrap her in a towel, we can smile and coo to our heart's content. But we dare not make too little of this. It is more than a family ceremony, more than a congregational celebration, though it is those things. Baptism marks the start of the Christian life; it gives us our identity. We are named as God's own, marked with the sign of Christ, given a vocation, and empowered for the living of our lives. It is more than a singular event; it is the beginning of a journey that takes a lifetime, a journey complete only in death.[11] It is a profound thing God does here: "Christ the water, incarnating God's water of creation, flows continuously in the Spirit, who waters the believers, who themselves become the spring of living water in the world."[12] In the presider's gestures, words, and tone—and in the congregation's participation (more on this in the next chapter)—is reflected awe and thanksgiving at nothing less than a miracle of grace.

Gesture and Blessing

In the preceding chapter we discussed the power of speaking blessing; here we turn to the enactment of that blessing. There are various models for how one extends the arms during a benediction: one arm extended forward, two arms suspended above the congregation, one arm bent with three fingers extended to symbolize the Trinity. While there is certainly no one correct posture to assume for the benediction, there are plenty of methods to avoid. More than one acquaintance familiar with life in postwar Germany has noted that extending one arm forward with the palm upright, is eerily reminiscent of Hitler's infamous stance; such a benediction posture would not be received as blessing in that country. My students and I are continually building a repertoire of what not to do with one's benediction arms. Postures to avoid include the goalpost stance (arms raised at the sides at right angles), the superhero posture (imagine Superman taking flight), and the sprinkling of fairy dust (arms akimbo, fingers wiggling lightly). You may want to try out these various stances while looking in the mirror.

Some suggest the arms of the one giving a blessing ought to look as if the presider is giving the congregation one huge embrace. While there is a sweet sentiment behind that, the benediction is only partly about the relationship between presider and people. It may be more helpful to think of the presider laying hands on the congregation. In this stance, one or both arms are fully extended, held somewhat above the people and somewhat around them, in a gesture that communicates inclusiveness and is also reminiscent of the way we pray when we are calling down the Spirit upon a sister or brother.

It is important to remember that the one who pronounces blessing does so out of a sense of authority—not authority over the community, but *for* the community. Having just preached the word or prayed at the Table, the presider has led the assembly through the divine dance that is the worship of God. As the people prepare to be sent by God into the world, they wait for a word of blessing—a word that *empowers* them but does not *overpower* them[13]—a word that sends them forth assured of the providence and faithfulness of God. This blessing is not only a word—presiders also convey it by their tone, their eye contact, their facial expression, with their whole bodies.

The Art of the Gesture

The lifting of a hand or the extending of the arms both seem like such small things. Yet learning the gestures of worship is something of an art. A music reviewer for the *New York Times* notices "the consummate and subtle technique" of octogenarian pop star Tony Bennett, devoting an entire article to the way the singer uses gesture to communicate the meaning of the songs he sings. For clues of what the songs are about, he says, "You look at his hands and gauge the timbre of his voice." In "Maybe This Time," after singing "the pitifully hopeful epithets, 'Mr. Peaceful, Mr. Happy,' he raised an open hand and sang 'that's what I want to be,'" as if to say that such a condition is a privilege and not a right. As he began the song "I Left My Heart in San Francisco," Bennett "folded his arms as if about to deliver a history lecture" and sang "the glory that was Rome is of another day." This gesture implied "This is the moment . . . where you start trusting the protagonist of the song." The reviewer describes one last genius-filled move:

> And in Alan and Marilyn Bergman and Michel Legrand's "How Do You Keep the Music Playing?," as he sang the counterintuitive line "the more I love, the more that I'm afraid," he did something so quickly it was nearly subliminal. It was a slight shoulder shrug; a half-swivel of the wrists so that the left thumb is pointed to 10 o'clock and the right thumb to 2 o'clock; eyebrows raised and eyes looking downward. It meant: This might be hard to understand, but stay with me.[14]

To be sure, singing classic American pop songs is somewhat different than presiding in worship. Yet something of the art that Tony Bennett has perfected is part of presiding well. There is a grace involved, an attention to communicating with one's hands what one is voicing with one's words. In fact, what one does with one's face, eyes, hands, even the whole body, creates a presence and communicates meaning.

Imagine a presider saying, "The grace of our Lord Jesus Christ be with you," while looking down at his notes. Or, as some have observed, "If a presider were to say, 'Lift up your hearts' while turning pages in the book, then no hearts would be lifted." Attending to gesture is not just about being artful, however. What the presider does enables—or disables—the community's worship. "Grace in movement and reverence in touch are not 'put on' just for the liturgy: They are honest reflections of a person's life, of a person's awareness of the presence of God in all creation."[15] These small gestures communicate worlds about the grace of God, the faith and humility of the presider, and love and care for the whole worshiping body.

Gestures of the Whole Assembly

At this point it is helpful to acknowledge that gesturing is not the purview of the worship leaders only. Every worshiper can embody the words of worship through gesture and movement. There are some traditions, of course, whose worshipers gesture and move quite freely, raising hands in praise. There are others of us, however, for whom worship has been a rather sedate endeavor. I do not mean to make Pentecostals out of Presbyterians or impose a regimen of liturgical dance upon each worshiper, but I have discovered that even small changes in posture, even little gestures, can move me toward greater worship. When I am seated and another is praying aloud, I practice holding my hands open in my lap. I put both feet flat on the floor to remind myself that we are talking to God, the very creator of the cosmos, and that this is an astonishing and humbling thing. Sitting this way, with open hands, I remember that prayer is about relinquishing my own will as well as listening for God's answer. Both of those require a posture of receptivity, and the open hands help me to remember.

There are other small things that make a difference. When the presider says, "The Lord be with you," I extend my own hand when we all say, "and also with you," and find myself more actively engaged. Sometimes, if I am presiding within a community that I know well, I will ask them to stand with me and pray in the *orant* position, all of us standing together with arms wide and open hands, all of us raising up that prayer together.

In the now-classic documentary *This Is the Night*[16] the whole congregation stands during the prayers of blessing for those soon to be baptized. As the presider and sponsors go from one person to the next, laying hands on the candidates and praying for each of them individually, every member of the congregation raises his or her arms in a gesture of blessing, hands open as though they too were physically laying hands. By enacting their prayer bodily they create a sense of unity, and those who are farther removed from the action still feel connected. Imagine doing the same sort of thing when you are ordaining elders or deacons, or sending the youth of the church on a mission trip, or praying blessing upon confirmands. Think of the many people in the congregation who have strong and intimate connections with those receiving the blessing, and how much more part of the prayer they, and those for whom they pray, might feel.

Through simple gestures, a congregation's prayer is strengthened, and bonds of unity are made firm. And it is not only gesture, but also touch, that does this. When bread is shared, hands touch; when the cup is shared, eyes meet. When we greet one another, lay hands on one another, mark one another with ashes or oil, we pray without words, and our souls are enlarged.

Touch

It may seem unusual to speak of touch in worship, but in fact it is all through liturgy. In his classic book *Elements of Rite*, Aidan Kavanagh explains that

> the liturgy also has traditionally placed high priority on the human sense of touch. A touch of a human hand, an embrace, the bathing and anointing of bodies all speak volumes about the assembly's confidence in things and people and in the commerce by which human and divine reality is constructed. For with touching without words goes an immense and risky ambiguity—an ambiguity which allows escape from the tyranny of words and texts and safe expectations, howsoever briefly.[17]

This sort of language can make some of us very nervous. It must be acknowledged that in North American culture, people have difficulty thinking of touch in nonsexual terms. Myriad cases of clergy sexual misconduct have raised our awareness—and our indignation—at the abuses that have been perpetrated on others. Yet we would be poorer as a community if we allowed the abuses of some to rob the rest of us of an inherently human part of worship. In services of baptism and confirmation, ordination and commissioning, healing and wholeness, to name just a few instances, touch is a crucial part of how we enact a living faith. Even as simple a gesture as sharing the peace of Christ involves the clasping of hands or embracing of one another. In fact, it is the gesture that is key here: whether we get along with each other or not— whether we even know each other—we express our unity and our common prayer for Christ's peace through touch.

As eloquent as our words may be, it is the sensation of touch that communicates beyond words when we lay on hands and pray for the empowering Spirit, or for healing. For in that touch we enact the bond with one another which we have in Jesus Christ through our baptism; we convey that no one of us goes through challenges or hardships alone; we act out, with our own bodies, the incarnational faith that we share. The transcendent God, who is so far beyond us, draws near to us through touch.

One day in the fall of 2008, along the Inside Passage of Alaska—home to native Americans of the Tlingit tribe—four elderly Tlingit women (who are also Presbyterian) gently laid a colorful robe around another woman and prayed for her healing. The robe was the work of their own hands. Even though they live in four different small towns, some quite remote, they joined forces to create a healing robe for Presbyterians in their region. "The robe itself will not heal," explains one of the women, Rosie Fay (K'ool K'aa tl is her Tlingit name). "The robe represents the arms of Jesus Christ holding you close as it is put around you. The robe lets our Christian brothers and sisters know that they are loved."[18] The black, white, and crimson robe bears the images of an eagle and a raven—symbols of two branches of the Tlingit tribe—as well as the Presbyterian seal and every text in the Bible that tells of healing.

The day the robe was presented by the women, person after person came forward, each one enveloped in the robe and prayed over. The women knew the magnitude of the suffering in the southeast region of Alaska. The abuse of alcohol and drugs is rampant; domestic violence and disease follow. Even as the women themselves endured illness and hardship, they created the robe because they knew the healing power of prayer. It is to be passed among any of those in the Presbytery of Alaska who need it; each person who wears it is to place in the robe's inner pocket a note with his or her name and the date and place where prayers were held, so that the robe's story is told wherever it goes. Certainly the words of the prayers murmured over those who wear it will matter; but perhaps worth even more are the physical touch of the robe and the hands that hold it.

Anointing for Service

Sometimes prayers for healing, as well as prayers for power, sustenance, or courage, involve anointing with oil. While Roman, Anglican, and some free churches have long practiced anointing, not all of us are familiar, or comfortable, with the practice. I have become convinced, however, that when anointing begins at baptism, it can have a powerful impact throughout a person's life. Imagine that after the water baptism has taken place, the newly baptized one is anointed with oil as the pastor speaks these words: "*N.*, child of the covenant, you have been sealed with the Holy Spirit and marked as Christ's own forever," followed by a prayer for the sevenfold gifts of the Spirit.[19] The oil may be poured over the head, or it may be used to trace a sign of the cross on the forehead. Now imagine the same person at the time of confirmation receiving the same sign of the cross traced in oil on her forehead.[20] She has seen that same gesture performed every time someone has been baptized, and so she connects her own profession of faith with her baptism and the promises that were made to and for her.

A few years later, she is commissioned with a number of other people from her church as they embark on a challenging mission. As she feels the cross traced, once again, on her forehead, she is reminded that in her baptism she has been claimed by God and given the gifts she needs for this work. Years pass, and she is ordained to an office in the church. People gather around her to lay hands upon her, and there is another anointing, and she remembers that the same Spirit given her in her baptism is being poured out upon her with new power. After a time, illness strikes. Again, people surround her to lay on hands, and she is anointed with oil. As she feels the touch on her forehead and smells the now-familiar aroma of the oil, she remembers that God has been with her on this journey ever since she was baptized, and that the One who claimed her then will not let her go now. All through a life, this simple ritual of touch can communicate layers of meaning.

The body remembers. You learn to ride a bicycle, and even after years of not riding, you remember how to do it. You learn to play one of Bach's two-part inventions on the piano when you are twelve years old and manage to still be able to play it (more or less) when you are forty. The clasp of a familiar hand not only gives momentary comfort but also carries in it the memory of years of companionship. The smell of a newborn baby brings to mind the feel and smell of your own newborn, now grown. And so the tracing of a cross, the scent of oil, the touch of water to the skin remind us, in ways that delve beneath the surface of our best explanations, of the covenant God has made with us.

There are few greater privileges than to lay hands on another, in anointing or ordaining or praying for healing. To touch a forehead, to hold a hand, to cradle a head while praying for the deepest physical and spiritual pains, to call on the empowering Spirit of God—all this is a remarkable and awe-inspiring thing. When a dear friend was ordained before her Baptist congregation, she knelt and a long line formed. One by one, people went to place their hands on her head and pray for her; the presence of the Spirit was palpable, and it was a blessing for us all to be part of this ritual that was both intimate and personal and yet connected to the transcendent power of God.

I once took part in a worship service led by a number of students at Columbia Seminary. They were from African American traditions, and one of them brought a small vial of oil. As the worship leaders gathered to begin the service, she asked each of us if we wanted an anointing. "Yes!" I practically shouted. And so she poured a bit of the oil into my hand and told me to place it on my mouth, or my throat, because I was to sing that day.

As I went to my place, I could smell the oil's scent, and my spirit calmed. This singing, I was reminded, was not about my skill, nor was it about pleasing or impressing anyone. It was all for God and God's people. As my breathing slowed, I was reminded that we were all in this together, and that God would provide the power required for whatever tasks were ours. To share in this simple anointing was to say, one Christian to another, "We are called to this." It was to say, "Remember Who this is about." It was to say, "You are given all the power you need."

When the time came to sing, it was as if the Spirit took my voice and led it to soaring; a current of electricity ran from my feet to the top of my head; and I experienced a kind of abandon I had never felt before. My singing was free, not for the purpose of self-expression, but so that God could use it. Not every experience of anointing is so dramatic, of course, which is a good thing—this is not some magical potion! Regardless of the sensations or emotions that may or may not accompany such a ritual, however, the act continues to be one through which God works.

Sara Miles tells the story of wanting to offer an anointing to the people who made their work at the St. Gregory Food Pantry possible, something that would make explicit the connection between prayer and work. Since the Food Bank staff and drivers were not free to come to the church, she went to them. She drove down to the warehouse, carrying a little vial of scented olive oil in her pocket. She felt a little shy about doing it, but she asked if anyone wanted a blessing. A man named Arthur, who was working with the food scales, said, "Yes! Oh yes!" A woman named Cynthia came over too, turning her palms up to receive the anointing. Eddie, the guy who drove the forklift, pulled up, tooting the horn. "Me too!" he called out. "I really need that."

"I looked at each of them in turn and took their hands," she writes, "soft, calloused, warm, damp—in mine. 'Arthur,' I said, dipping my thumb in the oil and making the sign of the cross on his palms, 'every time you touch someone with these hands, may you show them God's love. . . . Cynthia, in all the work you do with these hands, may God's mercy and justice shine forth. . . . Eddie, bless all the work of your hands, and may God keep you in his hands, safe and loved." They were a little embarrassed, a little touched. They didn't know quite what it all meant, but they knew it made a difference.

Miles goes on to say that as she went out into the city after that, she noticed people's hands—the hands that gave her a cup of coffee in the coffee shop—the "hands holding hands on the street or stroking a baby's face. Hands putting bread in a bag or opening a door and holding a broom and pouring water and touching a neighbor. *I noticed how marking a body as holy made holiness more visible.*"[21] Her story reminds us that a ritual not only affects us in the moment, but also changes the way we see, causing us to apprehend something more about what God is doing in the world.

Anointing for Healing

Theologian Don Saliers tells the story of a healing service at Saint John's Abbey, a Benedictine monastery in Minnesota. Everyone gathered for evening prayer, singing psalms and reading Scripture. Not only were the usual members of the community in attendance, but several others who lived in the monastery infirmary were there as well. The latter were seated in a circle of chairs in the midst of the gathering, and at one point the abbot invited all the others to come forward to lay hands on them. The abbot blessed the healing oils and anointed their hands and foreheads, then each person there walked slowly around the circle, touching each one who had been anointed and saying a simple word of blessing. "This took time," Saliers writes. "A slow adagio dance. A remarkable circle." As he neared one elderly man that he had known for years, he touched his hand tentatively. The elder reached out a gnarled hand and touched his face. "As we circled amongst the chairs," he recalls, "the double anointing continued likewise with others—many of whom I did not know—and the tears intermingled with the fragrance of the oil and the rhythm of this luminous dance of blessing."[22]

Saliers narrates a moving scene that speaks of the bonds of community and the power of touch. There are numerous models for services of healing and wholeness across Christian traditions, and space does not permit an in-depth survey of the variety of possibilities. What is constant, however, is the power of touch between one human and another, reminding us that the Word became flesh and dwelt among us, full of grace and truth.

Centuries ago Tertullian went so far as to say that these things are utterly crucial. "The flesh is the hinge of salvation [*caro cardo salutis*]," he said. "... For the flesh is washed that the soul may be cleansed; the flesh is anointed that the soul may be consecrated; the flesh is sealed that the soul may be strengthened; the flesh is overshadowed by the laying on of hands that the soul may be illumined; the flesh is fed by Christ's body and blood that the soul may fatten on God."[23] Indeed, God meets us in our flesh, touching us through one another, meeting us where we live and binding us continually into the body of Christ.

For Further Reading

Charles D. Hackett and Don E. Saliers. *The Lord Be With You: A Visual Handbook for Presiding in Christian Worship*. Akron, OH: Order of Saint Luke Publications, 1990.

Gabe Huck and Gerald T. Chinchar. *Liturgy with Style and Grace*. Chicago: Liturgy Training Publications, 1998.

Christopher Irvine. *The Art of God: The Making of Christians and the Meaning of Worship*. Chicago: Liturgy Training Publications, 2006.

Chapter 6

The Feet

Presiding in Sacred Space

*T*here once was a little girl with a big imagination. One day, as her mother worked, the girl, Annika, played at her feet, sorting through the scraps of cloth from her mother's sewing projects. She collected all the great, long pieces of cloth she could find, and then disappeared. After a rather long period of silence, her mother went looking for her. Eventually she found her outside, sitting in the grass. The girl had a long pole that she had found in the garage and was attaching the scraps of cloth to it with huge wads of tape. Her mother, naturally, asked her what she was doing. "Without taking her eyes from her work she said, 'I'm making a banner for a precession [*sic*]. I need a precession so that God will come down and dance with us.' With that, she solemnly lifted her banner to flutter in the wind, and she slowly got up to dance."[1] Children know the things we have forgotten: We need a procession! That is, we all need worship to incorporate some ritual forms, some common ways of moving and acting together. There is some instinct that urges us to act out what we believe, for believing is about living life with God before it concerns assenting to doctrinal formulations. The doctrine is important, of course, but it is not everything.

Admittedly, the word "ritual" sends some folks running in the opposite direction. For many in North American culture, "ritual" has come to mean "rote"—something repetitive, boring, and devoid of meaning. Yet ritual is not about mindless repetition of a set of words or gestures. Rather, it involves a community's shared practices that create space for God to break in, sometimes in surprising ways. "Our problem is not that we expect too little of ritual," opines Nathan Mitchell, but that we expect too much of it."[2] That is, we expect that rituals will somehow create meaning. The goal of liturgy, however, "isn't meaning but meeting," insists Mitchell. "And meetings are always risky. Christian worship is not doctrine disguised in ritual shorthand but action that draws us into the dynamic, hospitable, yet perilous space of

God's own life."[3] Or, as little Annika might put it, the rituals of worship invite God to dance with us.

In chapter 4 I mentioned the church of the Poor Clare Monastery in Lilongwe, Malawi, where the worshipers literally dance with God. In this church they process into the sanctuary with the Gospel book (the liturgical book from which the Gospel is read). Both women and men take part in the procession, as they dance toward the altar to the accompaniment of drumming and singing. When they reach the altar, they continue to dance around, singing all the while—the women dancing with their hands up and open, swaying rhythmically to and fro, the men dancing with palms forward, giving them a little shake from left to right, each dancing in patterns that are customary for Malawi women and men.

One of the women carries on her head a large clay pot wrapped in cloth. She dances in the women's circle until, at the appointed time, she places the pot on the altar and begins to unwrap the cloth. When the pot is uncovered, the Gospel book is drawn from it, and the whole community erupts into joyful ululations. This liturgy was originally designed for Christmas, and the clay pot symbolizes Mary's womb—when it is opened, it bears forth the Word of God, the Gospel book. There are layers of meaning at work here—through the movement of their bodies the worshipers carry forth the Word, "birthing" the Word-made-flesh as the pot is unwrapped and the book brought forth. They have not only accomplished the bringing in of the Scripture; they have also recounted one of the basic narratives of the faith.[4]

As Nathan Mitchell explains, "the body (Christ's and ours) not only *shows*; it *tells*—it is simultaneously *symbol* and *story*."[5] We have explored the symbolic nature of the body—of our identity as the body of Christ, of Jesus' body at work in the midst of humanity, of Christ's body broken in death and raised to new life, of his eucharistic body broken and shared at his table. Yet there is a narrative dimension to the body as well. In the rituals of worship, we tell the story of our relationship with God—in prayer and proclamation, in baptism and the Lord's Supper, we rehearse the gospel, the good news of God-with-us, past, present, and future.

In order to enact this story as well as tell it, the worshiping body requires space. One might say that worship space is primarily utilitarian—a shelter or meeting place, not holy in and of itself. It is the gathering of the people and their worship there that sanctify the space. So a gymnasium is just as legitimate a worship space as a cathedral. As the hymn asks,

What is this place where we are meeting?
Only a house, the earth its floor.

> Walls and a roof sheltering people
> Windows for light, an open door.

At the same time, however, liturgical space takes on meaning; just as the words we say and the rituals we share shape us as a people, so the space in which we enact our ritual life can form us, helping to give us our identity. And so the hymn continues:

> Yet it becomes a body that lives
> When we are gathered here,
> And know our God is near.[6]

The spaces in which we worship are holy because they are "places of encounter and ritual."[7]

Furthermore, the spaces in which we worship are public spaces, which means they take on a different character than, say, a bedroom or a living room. They are meeting rooms, yes, but the meetings that take place there happen around particular ritual acts—singing, praying, baptizing, preaching, sharing the Lord's Supper—and so the rooms take on a different quality than, say, an office conference room or the place where the school board convenes. The space reflects what happens in it. So, then, a Quaker meetinghouse reflects that body's ritual life: the seats may be positioned so all face the center, and there is no adornment save, perhaps, the beauty of the natural materials of wood or clear glass. The space is conducive to sitting and waiting for the Spirit to move someone in the community to speak. In traditions where preaching has been emphasized over the sacraments, the pulpit is often the strongest piece of furniture. In traditions where Eucharist is central, the table (or altar) is most prominent. Liturgical space, then, both reflects and continues to form the theology and practice of the group that meets there. The cycle is continuous.

The places in which we worship are set apart for particular actions, then, but they are not only "destinations, they are also *passages*," insists Robin Jensen. "The church space marks out the pilgrim's itinerary as well as points to the pilgrim's goal."[8] Through encounters with the space and the places in that space around which worshipers gather, people are led throughout a lifetime, from birth to death, from this earth to the heaven that awaits. People enter this sacred space, and they are drawn from the periphery to the center, carried through the transitions of life. Gathering around pulpit, font, and table, we are changed. For this reason Louis-Marie Chauvet calls liturgical space "transitional," because it is the place where we work out our relationship with God in prayer.[9]

The space in which we worship, and what we do together in it, can influence powerfully the life of faith. In considering what happens in worship space in general, and the presider's role in particular, it is helpful to consider the various sorts of liturgical spaces and centers, acknowledging that they appear to different degrees in different contexts.[10] First, there is gathering space, where people come together and greet one another as they move from the everyday world to worship, where they again meet as the body of Christ. Equally important is space for congregational movement—that is, enough room for people to make their way to their places, to move about for the offering and Communion, for processions, weddings, and funerals. Baptismal space (though often overlooked or neglected) ideally includes not only a font or baptistry with ample water, but also room for people to gather around. Similarly, a sanctuary needs space for Communion, with room enough not only for the presider but also for all who wish to gather at the Table. (A fuller discussion of sacramental spaces and congregational movement appears below.) In addition, three liturgical centers will occupy our attention in discussing the art of presiding: the pulpit (also called an ambo in some traditions), the baptismal font, and the Communion table.

In decades past, worship services were led primarily from the pulpit. While the trend in some churches today is to leave the pulpit to preach, much of the rest of the service is still conducted from that spot. Increasingly, however, congregations are finding meaning in using all three liturgical centers—pulpit, font, and table—as places from which to lead various parts of the service.[11] This not only adds variety to the service but, more important, presiding from the font and table as well as from the pulpit reminds the worshiping body what lies at the heart of our identity and vocation as Christians. Because of the layers of meaning associated with the sacraments, there are numerous possibilities for presiding at font and table, providing rich opportunities for making connections between what we do in worship, what God is doing in our midst, and what God calls us to do in the world. We will explore these possibilities, but first we turn our attention to the pulpit.

The Pulpit

It has become an increasingly popular practice among preachers to eschew the pulpit altogether. Some claim that preaching from the pulpit distances them from their congregations, because they are raised too high above the ground or are set back at too great a length. Others feel that the pulpit, especially if it is a large one, is an obstacle that separates them from the people. Still others feel physically encumbered when they preach behind a pulpit, insisting that their animated styles require more space to move about. It is certainly true that sometimes the architectural styles of sanctuaries can impede what congregations, and presiders, hope to do in worship, and communities must figure out how to overcome, or work around, the building they have inherited.

I would suggest, however, that in many, if not most, cases, the pulpit ought to be reclaimed as sacred space, for there is symbolic power in where we put our bodies. At its most basic, the pulpit is a place for the Bible to rest. Consider, for example, this scene. The reader for the day stands up and walks to the center of the platform, takes a piece of paper out of his pocket, unfolds it several times, and begins the Scripture reading for the day. What is communicated here? The Word seems transitory, even disposable. One would not be able to tell whether the reader was about to read from holy texts or recite his grocery list. Now imagine that the Bible—a beautifully bound, large book— rests on a stand, having been brought there, perhaps, at the opening of worship by one of the children of the congregation. This time the reader makes her way to the place of the Word, and reads not from a slip of paper, or even from her own personal Bible, but from the book that belongs to the whole community. Something different is communicated here: the Word is not our personal possession, but a gift to, and for, the whole body. Furthermore, there is a sense that the Word is not at our disposal but, rather, that we bring ourselves to the Word. When the pulpit is the place for both the reading of Scripture and the proclamation of that Word, then that space is open to those who would read or preach. A place for the Bible becomes not just beautiful and convenient storage, then, but a space to enter, and a symbolic reminder throughout the entire service of the presence of the Word—in Scripture and in the person of Jesus Christ—in our midst.

If that language sounds sacramental, it is. In the same way that the table is the place set aside for the celebration of the Lord's Supper, and the font is the place set aside for baptism and its related rites, the pulpit is set aside for the sacrament of the Word. In arguing for the importance of the sacraments, John Calvin compared them to the Word: "Therefore, let it be regarded as a settled principle that the sacraments have the same office as the Word of God: to offer and set forth Christ to us, and in him the treasures of heavenly grace."[12] Or, to put it conversely, the Word of God—understood as Scripture read and proclaimed—has the same office as the sacraments.

Calvin taught that the Word is as food to us. To the psalmist, God's word is like honey. Wisdom serves up a feast of bread and wine. Jesus is born in Bethlehem (a word meaning "house of bread") to give himself as the bread of life. As he teaches, he feeds, multiplying bread like manna in the desert.

He cooks up Easter breakfast on the beach. He reveals himself on the road to Emmaus in the breaking open of the Word and in the breaking of bread. He who is the Word is shown forth in words as well as in meals. It is no wonder, then, that Augustine and then Calvin—to name just two—saw Word and Sacrament not as two separate entities but as two parts of one whole. That is, the word is sacramental, as Christ is made present in the reading and proclaiming of Scripture. And the sacrament proclaims Christ crucified and risen even as he is made known to us in ways that go beyond our words and understanding through the breaking of bread and pouring of wine. It follows, then, that just as Eucharist requires a place for the meal, proclamation requires a place for the food of the Word.

I have come to the conclusion that few circumstances warrant a preacher's abandoning the pulpit. Presiders who preach from the floor of the sanctuary can seem cold and distant, just as those who proclaim from the pulpit are able to exude warmth and compassion. If the pulpit makes preachers uncomfortable, it may not be an altogether bad thing, for proclamation of the Word is not a task for the fainthearted. One approaches preaching with fear and trembling; who are we to think that we might have a word from the Lord? It is only by the empowerment of the Holy Spirit that we are able to speak—and only because of the grace of God that we are allowed to go through with it.

Those of us who insist on roaming about the front of the sanctuary as we preach, in the name of being more approachable or accessible, run the risk of taking preaching less seriously than we should. This is not to say that the gospel has never been preached outside the pulpit. But it is to say that it is difficult for this form of preaching to convey that God is the focus of the proclamation at hand, for it is only the preacher who is visible now. This preacher may be charismatic, genuine, sincere, and inspiring, but when proclamation mimics the form of a late-night television monologue, then preaching becomes more about the preacher's performance ability than about the Word of God; the people must work harder to see Christ, and not the preacher. Entering into the sacred space of the pulpit does not separate the preacher from the congregation if that preacher understands himself to be called forth from the midst of the body and entrusted with the holy, terrifying privilege of going to the deep wells of Scripture and proclaiming the good news of God. There is something at stake here, and it has more to do with an encounter with the holy than it does with the performance skills of the preacher.

Finally, as much as we may like to think of ourselves as indispensable, pastors come and go. We preach and baptize and celebrate the Lord's Supper for a length of time, in a particular place. But we are but temporary occupants of the office. Other ministers preceded us, and others will follow. In some churches, other pastors share the space with us. Yet the Word of God stays constant, and the sacred places of table, font, and pulpit serve as reminders of that truth. "The grass withers, the flower fades; but the word of our God will stand forever" (Isa. 40:8).

Leading from the Font

In imagining what parts of worship might be led from the baptismal font,[13] it is helpful to recall the various meanings, or metaphors, of baptism. In baptism we are washed clean; dying with Christ in the waters of baptism, we are raised to new life with him. Through the waters of baptism we are delivered from slavery to freedom. We are incorporated (or initiated, or grafted) into the body of Christ, bound to one another in a community of equality where there is no Jew nor Greek, no slave nor free, no male nor female. Reborn in the waters of baptism, we are birthed from the womb that is the font. We are refreshed and renewed by living water, our thirst for God quenched along the way until we reach the city of God, where the river of life will flow without ceasing. Gifted with the Spirit, we are strengthened for the journey and empowered for the life of discipleship to which we are called.

Throughout the course of any given worship service, these meanings and metaphors might be recalled by leading an element of the service from the baptismal font. As the presider (a minister or a member of the congregation) calls the people to worship, he or she reminds them of their identity as the baptized people of God. By standing at the font, the connection between who we are and why we gather is made more visible. While the words used to call the people to worship do not need to be explicitly baptismal, they may point to an element of our identity. Consider this text, for instance, which focuses on the activity of the Holy Spirit:

> The Spirit is in this place—
> birthing new life,
> illumining our hearts,
> enflaming our desire for justice,
> renewing our love.
>
> Come worship the Spirit,
> God, Three in One,
> who lives and moves among us.

Here, the people are reminded of the ways that the Spirit, given in baptism, continues to work in their lives and are urged to worship the triune God. The presider may simply stand by the font, or she may touch the water, lift water from the font, or pour it into the font. Any of these acts will help to draw people's attention to the baptism that binds them into one body.

The sequence beginning with the call to confession and ending with the declaration of forgiveness (and the expression of praise that may follow) may also be led from the font. The possibilities here are rich, given the associations between baptism, cleansing, and forgiveness. Again, the presider may pour water (if it has not already been done at the beginning of the service), touch it, lift it, or simply stand beside the font. Scripture provides ample texts for calling people to confession, such as these words adapted from Hebrews 10:22:

> Let us draw near to God with sincerity of heart
> and full assurance of faith,
> our guilty hearts sprinkled clean,
> our bodies washed with pure water.
>
> Together, let us confess our sins
> before God and one another.[14]

Sometimes words other than those from Scripture can be used as well, provided they are faithful to what the church believes about baptism:

> Come to the waters,
> you who long to be renewed;
> come to the waters,
> you who ache to be healed;
> come to the waters,
> you who yearn to be reconciled to God and one another.
> Redemption is near for all who call on the name of the Lord.

After the congregation prays a prayer of confession, the presider proclaims the promised forgiveness of God. Again, Scripture provides dynamic language, as that heard in Romans 6:

> Because we were buried with Christ in these waters,
> we are raised to new life with him.
> I declare to you, in the name of Jesus Christ,
> we are forgiven.

Language that echoes, but does not quote, Scripture also can be evocative:

> Hear the good news!
> God's mercy is poured out like a mighty river,
> grace flows like an never-ending stream.

> Believe the gospel, and give thanks!
> In Jesus Christ, we are forgiven.

It is also possible to use words that do not refer explicitly to baptism by calling attention to the water. In this case, the presider pours water into the font after saying, "Hear the good news!" allowing ample time for the pouring to be seen and heard:

> Hear the good news! [*pour*]

> The saying is sure and worthy of full acceptance,
> that Christ Jesus came into the world to save sinners.

> He himself bore our sins
> in his body on the cross,
> that we might be dead to sin
> and alive to all that is good.

> I declare to you in the name of Jesus Christ,
> we are forgiven.[15]

Certain days or seasons of the year might suggest particular language for declaring forgiveness, such as this text prepared for Christmas Eve or Christmas Day:

> Hear the good news!
> The one who was born of Mary
> has delivered us from the waters of this womb,
> the fount of rebirth,
> in order to save us and set us free.
> Friends, believe the unbelievable news!
> In Jesus Christ, we are forgiven.

The imagery here is vivid, reminding the people of Christ's own humanity and his identification with ours, as well as the Spirit's gift of rebirth in baptism.

In all these examples, we see how both our understanding of confession and forgiveness and our understanding of baptism are broadened. As one wise pastor has put it, confession is "not just about dredging up the week's sins and presenting them to God for forgiveness. It's about being washed clean, given a fresh start, rescued from drowning, set free from bondage. It's about living into a new life, living out our baptism, remembering the grace that has claimed us and the life to which it calls us."[16]

Rites related to baptism, such as confirmation, ordination, and the reception of new members, may appropriately take place around the baptismal font.

When young people who have been baptized as infants make a profession of faith, standing around the font makes vivid the connection with baptism. In baptism they were claimed by God, and God said yes to them before they were able to respond. Now, however, they *can* respond, saying yes to God and giving thanks for the promises made for them by their parents. Ordination or commissioning can also take place near the font, reminding everyone present that these people are living out in particular ways the vocation given to all Christians in baptism, and recalling that the same Holy Spirit that has been at work in them since baptism is at work in them in this phase of life as well. And certainly, when Christians from another community join in fellowship with our own, we gather around the font, mindful that we are already sisters and brothers in Christ through our common baptism. (The Presbyterian *Book of Common Worship* and the *United Methodist Book of Worship* both contain liturgies for these occasions that are clearly associated with the baptismal rite.) Similarly, whenever the Apostles' Creed is spoken (the creed associated with baptism), it may be led from the font by the presider or a member of the congregation.

Finally, the sending might be done from the font, drawing attention to the vocation of all the baptized to live as Christ's body in the world. Again, the presider may lift the water from the font and let it fall, or simply stand beside the baptismal waters to help make the connection clear. He may use a charge that echoes biblical language, such as Matthew's injunction to "Go out into the world in peace. Love the Lord your God with all your heart, with all your soul, with all your mind; and love your neighbor as yourself," or Micah's reminder that "God has shown you what is good. What does the Lord require of you but to do justice, and to love kindness, and to walk humbly with your God?"[17] Or one might speak a charge that makes explicit the baptismal connections with the life of discipleship, such as the charge mentioned in chapter 3:

> You who have been born of water
> and anointed with the Holy Spirit,
> go forth from this place,
> following wherever God may lead,
> to show forth Christ's light to the world.
> And as you go, remember
> that whatever is required of you,
> your baptism is sufficient for your calling.

Speaking words such as these from the font communicates that "we are being sent to live our baptism in the world, dying to self, trusting day by day that we will be raised in Christ to new and abundant life."[18] The waters of baptism remind us that Christ himself sends us forth to be his body in the world. And the benediction that follows assures us that the God who claimed us in baptism remains with us always, sustaining and empowering us through the work of the Holy Spirit, as we step out "once more on this unknown, risky, glorious, difficult, scary, joyful, magnificent adventure, as disciples of the crucified and risen Savior."[19]

Leading from the Table

In addition to presiding at the Lord's Supper, there are opportunities for leading other parts of the worship service from the table. Just as we might call people to worship from the font, we might also call them from the table, pointing to our identity as a eucharistic people.

> People of God, come!
> Come feast on God's Word,
> be filled at Christ's own table,
> and sing out your praise
> as we gather around the signs of unfathomable grace.

Or, we might call people with language that reflects both baptismal and eucharistic language. These words from Isaiah 55:1, for instance, do just that:

> Ho, everyone who thirsts,
>   come to the waters;
> and you that have no money,
>   come, buy and eat!
> Come, buy wine and milk
>   without money and without price.
>
> God has made an everlasting covenant with us.
> Praise the Lord!

Similarly, these words echo several biblical themes and point to our identity as people of the font as well as the table:

> Come and be renewed by living water.
> Come and be fed at the table of the Word.
> Come to eat the bread of life
>   and drink the cup of salvation,
>   for Christ is waiting to meet us here.
> Alleluia! Praise the Lord.

Words such as these spoken from the table can be particularly effective if they are heard after the people watch the symbols of worship being brought in, a task that might be entrusted to some children in the church, to take place during opening music, or the first hymn, or the singing of a simple, cyclic song.[20] One child brings in the community's Bible and places it on the pulpit; one child brings in a pitcher of water and pours it into the baptismal font; one or two others bring in a cup and plate (with bread, if Communion is being celebrated; empty if it is not) and set them on the table. Here, the whole community has watched—without words—the bringing forth of the primary symbols around which we gather. Then, when the presider (again, the minister, or any member of the congregation, including a child or youth) speaks words about water and word and bread, the body apprehends the richness of what it is we do when we come together for worship.

The prayers of the people afford another opportunity for leading from the table. Even when Eucharist is not being celebrated,[21] the table symbolizes a gathering place, the place where the people come to pray. This is the family table around which we share joys and fears, hopes and desires, where we pray for one another, for the church, and for the world. If the pulpit is the place for proclamation, the table is the place for prayer—for giving thanks, for lamenting, for interceding, for supplicating, for affirming our trust that Christ will come again.[22] As Marney Wasserman puts it, this praying "is sacramental work, embodying in loving acts the love and grace we know in Jesus Christ."[23]

Similarly, the offering and thanksgiving may be led from the table. We give of ourselves and our lives to God, an embodied way of giving thanks. "The earth is the Lord's and all that is in it," we proclaim, "the world, and those who live in it."[24] We return to God the gifts of the earth and all with which we have been entrusted, even our very selves. This, too, has sacramental echoes. To call forth the offerings of the people from behind the table is to recall the gifts offered at Communion as well as the gifts given to us there— God's own self-giving. Some have suggested that the prayer of thanksgiving might even reflect the shape of the eucharistic prayer, even if Communion is not celebrated, for this pattern leads us through a fulsome prayer of thanks— for all God's mercies, for the work of Jesus Christ, for the gift of the Holy Spirit, who enables us to live lives of service.[25]

Finally, the sending might also be done from the table. Imagine that the worshiping body has celebrated Communion that day—the people have been fed from the table of the Word and the table of the Meal, strengthened and encouraged, met by Christ himself. After the presider gives thanks for the miracle and mystery of that meal and asks that the people might be sent out to live faithfully—and after the congregation has sung a hymn that will carry them forth—the presider then charges the people, saying, "Go now to love and serve the Lord, the body of Christ for a hungry world." The connection between being fed at the eucharistic table and feeding other hungry people is made clear. Christ gives us his body, that we might in turn be his body for the world.

Moving through the Liturgy

We have discussed where the presider might stand for various parts of the service, but have not yet touched upon getting from one place to another. The key here is not to prescribe some set of highly regimented movements, but rather to suggest a habit of intentionality and style. Just as there are no throwaway words in liturgy, so there are no throwaway movements. Standing, walking, and even sitting require our attention.

Imagine, for instance, a presider who slumps in her chair while someone else is in a leadership role, or one who crosses his legs and flings an arm over the back of his seat. Those postures would not only communicate a lack of attentiveness, but even a lack of respect for whatever is going on in the service. Keeping the feet flat on the floor, or perhaps crossed only at the ankles, helps to convey that the presider is engaged in what is happening, especially when the face and even the body are inclined toward the action. The hands ought to rest comfortably in the lap, refraining from fidgeting, shuffling papers, cleaning nails, and so forth.

Standing seems like a straightforward-enough thing, but even here a bit of self-awareness is useful. Standing in worship is different from standing in line for tickets at the movie theater or standing by the hors d'oeuvres table at a party. You are on holy ground! Try to avoid tugging at your stole or fussing with your sleeves; once you are dressed and vested, let it be. If you are anything like me, you may have a tendency to sway or shift your weight from one foot to another. These can be distracting movements, so it is probably best to try to maintain a still—but not rigid—posture. Again, if you are attending carefully to the action in the service, even if you are not the one on whom the attention is focused, most of this will take care of itself, and you will be signaling a posture of attentiveness to the rest of the congregation.

The act of walking from one place to another in front of a room full of people can strike fear into the hearts of otherwise well-balanced people. Prop me up and let me sing in front of a thousand folks, and I am just fine. Ask me to walk across the front of the sanctuary, or climb two steps into a pulpit, and

I am a nervous wreck. There is a reason why I had more knee scars than most by the time I was ten! The key to moving in the liturgy is to be purposeful; if you are headed to the table, look there in anticipation. If you are taking part in a procession, look forward and not down, since you move not only your own body but also the attention of the whole worshiping body toward the liturgical centers of the church. Again, this is holy ground; to be leading the people in worship is a privilege that evokes awe, humility, and deep joy.

It is helpful to think through the choreography of a service beforehand with all those who are participating in the leadership. If one is leading the confession sequence from the font, when should she move to that place, and when should she return to her seat? If there is a period of silence following a reading of Scripture, should the reader remain standing in place for that period of time? Thinking through these questions in advance is not just good stage management; when every person knows what to do and when to do it, then a sense of unity is conveyed, and worshipers are able to trust those in leadership without anxiety.

Finally, all movement, gesture, and speech ought to be in proportion to the space. It makes a difference whether you are leading a congregation of eight hundred worshipers or a gathering of twenty-five. Each setting requires the same degree of planning, the same careful attention to detail, the same degree of engagement, the same amount of love. In all contexts, think about the size of your movements and the volume of your voice (with or without amplification) in relation to the worship space.

Movement of the Congregation

Ideally a congregation's worship space is ample enough to allow for easy movement of the people. The worshiping body needs room for gathering, processing, sharing the peace of Christ, dancing, singing, baptizing, communing, and the laying on of hands. Many congregations worship in spaces with pews packed so tightly that movement is difficult. (Pews, incidentally, were a late medieval invention. Before the fourteenth century, public worship spaces were open and people stood, moving from place to place as the action of the service warranted.) Congregations that are fortunate to be able to build or renovate their sanctuaries have an opportunity to think about how the worship space can be designed to accommodate the congregation's movement. Some churches opt for flexible seating (i.e., chairs or shorter pews) that can be arranged in a variety of patterns, allowing worshipers to see one another and to be gathered around the primary liturgical centers.

Congregations that are working with their existing spaces sometimes elect to remove some front pews in order to create more room for gathering around Communion tables and baptismal fonts. Some churches are rethinking baptismal space altogether, placing large fonts at the entrance to the sanctuary, where people are reminded of their baptism whenever they enter. At best, these spaces are ample enough for the people to gather around at the time of a baptism. This is a significant development, as it enables the worshiping body to enact what we believe—that baptism is an act of God in the midst of *the whole community*. When the congregation is able to gather around the baptismal font or baptistry, we wait as the body to receive our new member. When that one emerges dripping from the water, we can literally embrace and welcome her. Now baptism is not something that happens "up there" with the minister and a few others. We enact together what it is—the initiation into the whole body of Christ.

This same sense of gathering around the sacramental act is possible in Communion as well. At St. Giles Cathedral in Edinburgh—and closer to home at the Church of the Servant in Grand Rapids, Michigan—worshipers leave their seats for Communion and gather in a large circle around, or near, the Communion table. Bread and wine are passed from hand to hand as people share the body and blood of Christ with one another. This process is repeated several times until everyone is fed. In moving to the table, worshipers embody the gathering of people from east and west, north and south. In passing the bread and cup from one to another, they enact the sharing of a meal between all the baptized, looking at one another's faces as they take part in the feast. Certainly this is not the only way to celebrate Eucharist, but it is one way that enriches the body's experience of communion with Christ and with one another.

Not all congregations are in a position to renovate or build space. But every community can consider how to best use the space they have so that the whole worshiping body can take part as fully as possible in liturgy that is, indeed, the work of us all.

Moving from the Sanctuary into the World

The final movement for us to consider only begins in the sanctuary. As vital as worship is, we do it not primarily for our own sakes but for the sake of the world. To understand worship as an embodied event is to recognize that every act of worship points not only to how *we* might be more fully blessed, or bettered, or healed, but also to how the whole *world* might be brought to wholeness and completion. It is about no less than "the final, corporate destiny of humanity itself."[26] Nathan Mitchell goes so far as to say that Christian liturgy is like a musical score—that "liturgical scores" are valid only insofar as there is some exterior ethical response. "Christian liturgy begins as ritual practice, but ends as ethical performance. Liturgy of the neighbor verifies liturgy of the church, much as a composer's score makes *music* only through the risk of performance."[27] His words are a crucial reminder that when we worship, we are in a constant exchange with the divine, who saves us and then sends us out to take part in the ever-hastening reign of God.

So what does all this mean in practical terms? It means that singing praises becomes not just an element of worship, but also a way of life. All of worship, at its heart, is doxological and, rightly lived, so is all of life. We practice praise, so that even in the face of death we know what to say to God, even if we do not feel it—for the God who formed our inward parts, the God who claimed us in baptism, the God who sustains our every breath, does not leave us to our own devices. We practice confession too, for in adopting a posture of humility, in the confidence that God is merciful, we are more apt to extend grace to others, forgiving with a power that goes beyond our own will or power to do so.

We have already spoken of how baptism shapes us for living: in baptism we are given identity and vocation. And there is more: knowing that we have been initiated into a faith of equally beloved members, how can we judge or discriminate? Remembering our baptism, we are less apt to think too highly—or too critically—of ourselves, knowing that we have all been equally welcomed, equally redeemed, equally loved. Remembering our baptism, we strive to be living water for others.

The eucharistic table also shapes us for living in the world. We come hungry and leave filled, reminded of the goodness of God. We are strengthened for challenges that might otherwise seem overwhelming. And we are reminded that there are hungry bodies and hungry souls wherever we go. To *gather* as the body of Christ is also to be *sent* as the body of Christ—which, frankly, is no easy thing. Being fed at the table reminds us that we are utterly dependent on God's self-giving—that, in fact, all of humanity is equally dependent—and that the blessing of being fed requires from us that we strive to do justice, love mercy, and walk humbly with God.

In the end, everything we do together in worship is a way of leaning into the kingdom of God. "At the heart of it all," says Don Saliers, "Christian prayer and worship is the cry for God's will and covenant promises in Jesus Christ to be made real."[28] Whenever we pray the Lord's Prayer, we acknowledge this: "Your kingdom come, your will be done *on earth* as it is in heaven" (emphasis ours) is our way of saying that we know that when all is said and done, God will make everything right. And in the meantime we pray—we plead—that in whatever we say and do, God will somehow prepare the way, here and now, for Christ's coming.

Every gesture, every movement, every word involved in presiding must, at the heart of it all, communicate this conviction that in worship we keep alive the vision of the coming reign of God, enact it the best we know how, and trust the Spirit to equip us for living out that vision in our daily lives. This requires a deep spirituality as well as a well-honed theology, and it is to that topic that we now turn.

For Further Reading

William Seth Adams. *Moving the Furniture: Liturgical Theory, Practice, and Environment.* New York: Church Publishing, 1999.

Don E. Saliers. *Worship as Theology: Foretaste of Glory Divine.* Nashville: Abingdon Press, 1994.

Marney A. Wasserman. "Leading from Font, Table, and Pulpit." *Call to Worship: Liturgy, Music, Preaching, and the Arts* 40.4 (2007): 15–24.

Chapter 7

The Heart

The Spirituality of the Presider

*I*n Hebrew, the "heart" (*lēb* or *lēbāb*) is the center of being from which all action springs, as well as the beating organ in a person's chest. While many of us think of head and heart as being two separate, even competing, forces, the ancient Hebrews considered the heart to encompass the whole person: thought, feeling, and will.[1] In the fourth chapter of Proverbs, a parent instructs a child in how to be a wise person (4:20–27). The child is to listen carefully, to turn from "crooked speech," to keep the eyes looking forward and the path of the feet straight. And at the center of it all is the heart, from which flow "the springs of life" (4:23). Thus the writer of Proverbs sketches the anatomy of a wise person—eyes and ears, mouth, and feet—with the heart at its center.[2] One might say that this Hebrew understanding of the heart is also key for the wise presider, for at the core of it all, what we do with eyes and ears, mouth, hands, and feet springs forth from the heart. For all of the skill and practice we put into it, what dwells in the heart is the fount from which faithful presiding springs. To bring thought, feeling, and will to the act of presiding is to approach that work as a person of prayer who is committed to justice, abounding in compassion, and constantly seeking the will of God for the world, the church, and oneself. In spite of all the attention we necessarily give to what we do with eyes, ears, mouth, hands, and feet, presiding comes from the heart.

Presiding from the Heart

Presiding from the heart involves at least five essential practices, or ways of being. As we have mentioned, it is important that a presider prepares—that she knows the flow of the service and understands the internal logic and rhythms therein. Gordon Lathrop calls this knowing the liturgy "by heart." At

111

one level, this means committing portions of the service to memory. "There is a remarkable freedom in such knowledge," says Lathrop, "a freedom to begin to see that liturgy is not in the book but in the present actions of the assembly, a freedom to begin to invest the text with the gift of oneself."[3] The goal of this, of course, is not to be free to express oneself in the liturgy, for we know that leading worship is not about self-expression—but rather so that the texts might dwell in us, work on us, even change us. When that happens, we find "that the texts have begun to hold and carry" us.[4]

There is a declaration of forgiveness in the *Book of Common Worship*, for instance, that includes these words:

> Anyone who is in Christ
>   is a new creation.
> The old life has gone;
>   a new life has begun.[5]

Over the years, these words have become inscribed on my heart as well as my memory; I have become convinced, all the way down, that the Christian life is one of constant renewal, a continual turning and returning to God that, with the Spirit's help, enables us to forgive ourselves and one another. To claim such grace with deep gratitude changes the shape of a life and enables one to show grace to others. There are other words, too, like "Your kingdom come; your will be done on earth . . . ," that have a way of taking root in a heart as well, engendering hope in the reign to come and restoring courage for the work at hand. We are changed by these words as we live with them and live into them. One who presides from the heart imbues those words and their attendant actions with a depth of spirit that comes from allowing the words to abide within.

Furthermore, to know the liturgy by heart means understanding at a deep level what is happening in each element of the service, where that element in particular—and the service as a whole—is going. Aidan Kavanagh puts it well when he says that the presider "should know both the assembly and its liturgy so well that his [or her] looks, words, and gestures have a confident and easy grace about them. [He or she] presides not over the assembly but within it, . . . does not lead it but serves it."[6] If each service of worship is a journey, the presider is a guide, and every expedition goes better if the guide knows the way. This is not heavy-handed guidance though. It is more like what happens when geese take flight from a place of rest: one begins the honking signal, the rest pick up the song, and together the flock lifts off to ride the wind. When one knows well the patterns and rhythms of the service—knows them by heart—the congregation can take flight together.

Second, presiding from the heart means coming to worship as a person of prayer. Not only does this involve letting the prayers of the church (such as the Lord's Prayer) dwell within; it also means that the presider's work grows out of a deep well of personal prayer. To be a person of prayer is to be attentive to the people of the congregation, the community, and the world, and to hold those people in the heart when talking and listening to God. This involves some discipline of prayer, some solitude. Yet it also involves praying in common—that is, not on behalf of the assembly, but in and with the assembly. Over and over again I have heard ministers say, "I just can't worship when I'm leading worship!" I would be inclined to say that the inverse is true: one cannot lead worship without worshiping.

In order to worship while leading worship—or, to say it better, to lead worship as one who worships—a presider must practice letting go. After all the preparation is finished, after all the planning has been done, the time comes to loosen the tight grasp on it all and give it over to God. While this sounds like a "spiritual" thing, it has very practical implications. To give it over to God means trusting the people around us to do their parts well (and to cover it with grace when they do not). It also means trusting ourselves and all the hard work that has gone into preparing for a service, as well as forgiving ourselves when we make mistakes—which, of course, we will. As Aidan Kavanagh says in his inimitable style, "Reverence is a virtue, not a neurosis, and God can take care of [Godself]" if something goes wrong. In short, to worship while leading worship, one must put away fear and concerns about whether people will be impressed with us, or like us, or think well of us, and put our whole selves into worshiping God.

Third, presiding from the heart means loving and respecting the worshiping body with whom you gather. A faithful presider knows the people; she knows their lives, their struggles, their gifts, their pains. For all of the attention we must give to preparation, thoughtfulness, and style, at its heart presiding is full of hospitality and warmth, tempered with genuine reverence for the people and for the shared work of worship.

I know a pastor who served faithfully and well in the midst of the residents of a continuing care home for elderly people. She presided at the Sunday morning service, where most people were able-bodied and clearly engaged. There was another service in the afternoon, and many of the worshipers there were wheelchair-bound and not able to participate as fully as they once had, either mentally or physically.

On a Sunday when I was visiting, Communion was being served. The pastor, along with several others, circulated among the chairs and wheelchairs, distributing bread and grape juice to all who were there. The pastor approached one woman, hard of hearing and curled in upon herself, who could not figure out exactly what was going on. "Communion!" the pastor called out in a loud voice, "It's Communion!" Somehow this servant of the assembly, even while shouting, managed to convey grace and care. This is only possible from someone who loves. The words of Paul should never be far from the presider's mind:

> If I speak in the tongues of mortals and of angels, but do not have love,
> I am a noisy gong or a clanging cymbal.
> And if I have prophetic powers,
> and understand all mysteries and all knowledge,
> and if I have all faith, so as to remove mountains,
> but do not have love,
> I am nothing.
> If I give away all my possessions,
> and if I hand over my body so that I may boast,
> but do not have love,
> I gain nothing.
>
> (1 Cor. 13:1–3)

Love is at the heart of it all.

Fourth, those who preside from the heart must lead with authenticity, bringing all of our strengths and weaknesses, idiosyncracies and particularites, put forth as faithfully, humbly, and joyfully as we know how. A story told in the *New York Times* obituary for Pope John Paul II gives a lovely glimpse of what that sort of authenticity looks like. When Karol Wojtyla, the first non-Italian pope elected since 1523, stepped out onto the center balcony of St. Peter's Cathedral in Rome just after his election was announced, he faced a crowd that barely knew him and had trouble pronouncing his name. When they saw him they fell silent, and he surveyed them with tears in his eyes. At last he began to speak in accented Italian.

"I have come from a faraway country," he said, "far away, but always so close in the communion of faith." Cheers erupted here and there.

"I do not know whether I can express myself in your—our—language," he stammered, and the crowd laughed and cheered loudly.

"If I make mistakes," he said, smiling broadly, "you will correct me." The crowd went wild and the cheering grew and grew until the chant went up: "*Viva il Papa! Viva il Papa! Viva il Papa!*" With a simple gesture of humility and humor, he had won over an entire nation.[7]

It is that sort of grace that the best presiders bring to their work. While effective presiding does not rest on one's charisma or sense of humor, it does depend in part on allowing ourselves to be fully present, never hiding behind a cardboard cutout of what we imagine a good leader to be, but bringing our own wonderfully flawed selves to our work. We are freed from attempting to appear anonymous or faceless, saved from acting pompous or authoritative, liberated from the impulse to be entertaining or to force a falsely casual style. There is no need for a God-voice or for stilted gestures or holy postures. At the same time, the authentic presider recognizes that worship is a sort of drama—that the timing and tension and heightened activity involved in a service of worship requires a certain gravity, an unfailing sense of awe. To preside with authenticity, then, is not to bring our most natural selves, but our "best selves," to the task.[8]

Finally, to preside from the heart is to preside with passion. This does not mean bringing an overwrought sense of melodrama to presiding, but it does mean that our words and movements are imbued with the deep conviction that every bit of it matters. For at the root of all that presiders do is that vision of the coming reign of God—the vision that gathers us as the people of God, frees us for living the Christian life, and fuels us for working with God to help bring in the kingdom. Telling the story and enacting the gospel within the sanctuary walls forms us for living it out, the best we can, outside those walls, to live a life of love and to work for justice and peace and wholeness for one another and for all of God's children.

This is not just a personal passion, though; that is, we do not conjure it up on our own, out of our own sense of justice or the strength of our own convictions. We do not pray according to our own agendas or enthusiasms. Passion grows from allowing Christ to dwell within us, to invite "Christ, *the* leader of prayer, to live and move and be in us."[9] There is an abandonment of the self involved, an intentional submitting of our own wills to the will of Christ. The passion that undergirds our presiding, then, is not about us at all; rather, it is about being caught up in the vision of Christ's return and his promise to be at work in our midst, here and now, inviting us to be part of the amazing work of bringing in the reign of God. Our passion has nothing to do with self-expression, but with the miracles God is working, the glimpses of hope God is granting, within us, among us, and beyond us.

Presiders Are Made, Not Born

In every attentive worship leader who presides from the heart, an artfulness emerges. Over time skills are honed, rhythms become innate, instincts mature. The presider's style is neither too breezy nor too sober. And while the particularity of the person never disappears, the presider's personality never obscures the weighty joy of the tasks that the worshiping body has entrusted to him or her. None of this happens instantly. It is a process that takes time. So what does a new minister do—or one who has just begun to think about these issues? Consider the crab.

The Maryland blue crab (*Callinectes sapidus*, or savory beautiful swimmer) can only grow larger and more mature by shedding its shell and growing a new one. If you catch a crab and notice that the shell is still rather soft and that the underbelly of the shell is a lustrous, pearly white, then you know you have a crab with a new shell. You also know that there is a good deal of empty space inside that new shell (that is, not enough meat to make the labor-intensive work of picking a steamed crab worth your while), because the crab has not yet grown into it. It is best, then, to throw that lovely creature back into the water and let it mature until the new shell has hardened and become full of meat.

Maturing as a presider is something like growing crab-style. You learn the techniques, and think deeply about it all, and only gradually does it become part of you—that is, you construct a new shell of knowledge and skill, but it takes time to grow into that new shell. Will there be awkward moments? Yes. Will there be times of not quite knowing what to do or say? Certainly. But in time, the beautiful new shell strengthens, and one grows into it with fullness and richness.

Growing as a presider is not a solitary process, however. All of this honing of skills happens in the context of a real, live congregation, which means that none of it is abstract or hypothetical. If your speech is perfect, your intonations always expressive, your gestures evocative, your movements full of grace, and yet there is no connection with the people who have gathered to worship—indeed, if you are not, yourself, worshiping—then you have merely perfected some sort of liturgical performance art, which is of little value to a congregation and puts you at risk for missing the whole point. And yet, if you are attending to the people and their lives, listening for God in your own life, watching for God at work in the world—if you are genuinely praying with the worshiping body—well, then, that is a different story altogether. In fact, the people are the ones who mold a presider, if she or he is paying attention. As Robert Hovda put it, "No one is born a presider. No one is made a presider by training or talent or will or desire or anything but the choice of vocation and delegation of the faith community. There are certainly native aptitudes and basic training, but presiders, like all other ministers, are made by the church."[10] Thanks be to God for that.

Of course, to allow oneself to be shaped by the church requires a certain amount of humility. When I was a young pastor, the congregation in which I served would share prayer concerns before I led the prayers of the people. We allowed a fair amount of time for this—people stood and described people and situations for whom we were to pray, and then we all joined in prayer—and yet I never mentioned any of these concerns specifically in the prayer itself. Finally, a wise woman in the congregation pulled me aside after one Sunday morning service. She gently told me that the congregation would feel much more fully led in prayer if I actually prayed for the things they had mentioned. It seems quite obvious now—but then, I was afraid of leaving too much to chance. If I prayed for what had just been mentioned, I would have to leave my carefully crafted script. I would have to pray in the moment. I was terrified.

Of course, she was right. I could not learn to pray until I entered into the immediacy of prayer—until the words I offered embodied the cares of the people worshiping there, in that time and place. Yes, I could help to expand the boundaries of that prayer. Yes, I could think about the kinds of words to use, and how to shape the prayer. I could be well prepared. But in the end, I had to give myself over to prayer. Not every congregation shares concerns as part of the service. Yet even in congregations where prayer texts are prescribed, one must give oneself over to prayer, with and for these people and the world that we inhabit together.

There are other ways a congregation helps to form a presider. I remember a particular Sunday when I could do nothing right. I stumbled over every other word and forgot details left and right. It was if my brain was smothered in cotton and my limbs were encased in concrete. All I could hope for was an end to that service which, frankly, was nowhere in sight. And then I looked up to see a little girl in the congregation. She was child with difficulties—she struggled in school, she was large for her age and awkward, and she lacked the sort of filters that enable children to make good decisions about what sort of behavior is appropriate in public. Her emotions were always perilously close to the surface, and they would often get the best of her. She was also one of the most loving children I had ever met. On this particular Sunday, as I floundered through the service, she was watching me from her seat in the center of the congregation. When my eyes fell on her, she blessed me with a tremendous, beaming smile and gave me an enthusiastic thumbs-up. To see her was to hear the voice of God: "You are going to be OK. You are OK right now. This is all OK." She never knew the gift she gave me or that I would remember it years later.

The worshiping body forms us as presiders, in part by extending great big portions of patience to us. This same congregation put up with me for three or four years until I finally stopped shaking at the Communion table and was able to preside with some semblance of confidence. They endured my confusion about where Scripture should be read and when announcements should be made. They taught me about remaining faithful to God and to one another even through disappointment and tragedy and hurt. They made a pastor out of me.

The church does not, of course, work alone in this task of shaping presiders. The apostle Paul insisted that "the Spirit helps us in our weakness; for we do not know how to pray as we ought, but that very Spirit intercedes with sighs too deep for words" (Rom. 8:26). This is good news indeed, for even at our most technically skilled we are but hollow shells without the indwelling and outpouring of the Holy Spirit. The Spirit teaches us to pray, undergirding our stammering with holy breath. It is only through the working of that same Spirit that the Word is proclaimed—without the Holy Spirit, our preaching is gibberish, water merely makes us wet, bread and wine are simply appetizers for some other meal. But when the Holy Spirit is at work—and we trust it is so, praying continually for the same—then the Word is made present in the midst of the worshiping body, and new life is born again and again. This Spirit works through us, acts upon our embodied selves, coming to us in ways we can apprehend. John Calvin teaches that this is true for all Christians:

> Faith is the proper and entire work of the Holy Spirit, illumined by whom we recognize God and the treasures of his kindness, without whose light our mind is so blinded that it can see nothing; so dull that it can sense nothing of spiritual things. . . . First, the Lord teaches and instructs us by his Word. Secondly, he confirms it by the sacraments. Finally, he illumines our minds by the light of his Holy Spirit and opens our hearts for the Word and sacraments to enter in, which would otherwise only strike our ears and appear before our eyes, but not at all affect us within.[11]

If it is true for all Christians, then it is also true for presiders: we do nothing apart from the power of the Holy Spirit. If we do not first—and continually—give ourselves over to the Spirit in preparing for and carrying out the tasks of presiding, then we are simply learning the script and standing up to do a bit of playacting.[12] Yet here is the thing: when we do first—and continually—give ourselves over to the Spirit in preparing for and carrying out the tasks of presiding, then the Spirit does not disappoint. For when that happens, we are caught up in a power and movement that reaches so far beyond who we are and what we can do. We are lifted up and carried, enabled, and infused by the

Holy Spirit. We do not cease to be ourselves, yet we are not only ourselves, and certainly not only for our sakes, but we also listen and see, speak and move, for the sake of the worshiping body.

When All Is Said and Done

When all is said and done, it might be said that none of this matters. God is not limited by our lack of ability or faithfulness. As Annie Dillard famously commented, "A high school stage play is more polished than this service we have been rehearsing since year one."[13] And therein lies the humbling beauty of it all. Whatever gifts, whatever frailties, whatever convictions, whatever doubts, whatever it is that we bring, God gathers it up and blesses it and—praise be—grants us the unbelievable privilege of serving the worshiping body. Even though none of this is about us, we would be remiss if we did not say, "Thanks be to God," for allowing us the burdensome pleasure, the pleasurable burden, of presiding in the assembly.

And yet. There is a quality that is absolutely necessary. Call it faith, call it piety, call it spirituality; Hovda calls it "a personal belief that is real and meaningful and operative, and a disposition to prayer, especially prayer of praise and thanksgiving."[14] Whatever you call it, it is indispensible. Of course, presiders are susceptible to the same wonderings and questionings and doubts as any other Christian—and sometimes it is all right to struggle with those things with others who are walking the same path; yet to preside faithfully requires a confidence in the unfailing providence of God.

And at the heart of it all, a profound gratitude for all that is, and has been, and will be.

Notes

CHAPTER 1: CALLED OUT FROM THE BODY

1. Gordon W. Lathrop, *The Pastor: A Spirituality* (Minneapolis: Fortress Press, 2006), 6.

2. Gordon W. Lathrop, *Holy People: A Liturgical Ecclesiology* (Minneapolis: Fortress Press, 1999), 1.

3. Ibid., 21.

4. John Calvin, *Institutes of the Christian Religion* 4.1.9; ed. John T. McNeill, trans. Ford Lewis Battles, 2 vols., LCC (Philadelphia: Westminster Press, 1960), 2:1023.

5. Catherine Gunsalus González, "Some and All: Ordination and the Sacraments," *Reformed Liturgy and Music* 28.1 (Winter 1994): 4.

6. Ibid.

7. William Seth Adams, *Shaped by Images: One Who Presides* (New York: Church Publishing, 1995), 67.

8. Scott Haldeman, "Washed and Ready: Baptism as Call and Gift of Ministry," *Call to Worship: Liturgy, Music, Preaching, and the Arts* 40.2 (2006): 6.

9. Adams, *Shaped by Images,* 13.

10. Elaine Ramshaw, *Ritual and Pastoral Care* (Minneapolis: Augsburg Fortress, 1987), 22, as quoted in Adams, *Shaped by Images,* 14.

11. Benjamin Stewart, "Robert Hovda: Facing the Assembly," *Worship* 78.5 (Spring 2004): 428–29.

12. Gordon W. Lathrop, *Holy Things: A Liturgical Theology* (Minneapolis: Augsburg Fortress, 1993), 167.

13. Lathrop, *The Pastor,* 6.

14. Lathrop often speaks of a symbol being "broken" as a way of warning against any symbol being the last word. As weighty as the pastor's symbolic nature is, it must be mitigated by other powerful symbols, such as the community itself. As Lathrop puts it, "The content of the pastor's work, like the content of the Bible, the Eucharist, and Baptism themselves, must continually surprise these expectations, turning our religious hopes toward new references: the community gathered around the mercy of God in ordinary life; the community gathered around the life-giving cross; the community brought to new maturity in finding such mercy and life here, within our daily limits; the community open to the stranger and to a wider world in need of mercy and life; and that very mercy and life also given to the beggar-among-beggars who is the pastor. A pastor lives with symbols, is a symbol. But a profound spirituality for

pastors must involve a lifelong engagement with the reversals and surprises of these symbols."
The Pastor, 6.

15. Lathrop, *The Pastor,* 11.

16. Robert W. Hovda, *Strong, Loving, and Wise: Presiding in Liturgy* (Collegeville, MN: Liturgical Press, 1976), 67–68.

17. Lathrop, *Holy People,* 17.

18. Adams, *Shaped by Images,* 15.

19. Yme Woensdregt, "The Pastor as Liturgist," *Reformed Liturgy and Music* 30.4 (1996): 167–72.

20. Edward Farley, "A Missing Presence," *Christian Century,* March 18–25, 1998, 276.

21. Robert W. Hovda, "Liturgy's Many Roles: Ministers? . . . Or Intruders?" in *The Amen Corner,* ed. John F. Baldovin (Collegeville, MN: Liturgical Press, 1994), 154.

22. Ibid., 154–55.

23. Hovda, *Strong, Loving, and Wise,* 34.

24. Talal Asad, "Remarks on the Anthropology of the Body," in *Religion and the Body,* ed. Sarah Coakley (New York: Cambridge University Press, 1997), 48.

CHAPTER 2: THE EMBODIED NATURE OF WORSHIP

1. John Calvin, *Institutes of the Christian Religion* 4.14.18; ed. John T. McNeill, trans. Ford Lewis Battles, 2 vols., LCC (Philadelphia: Westminster Press, 1960), 2:1294–95.

2. Gordon W. Lathrop, *Holy People: A Liturgical Ecclesiology* (Minneapolis: Fortress Press, 1999), 17.

3. William Seth Adams, *Shaped by Images: One Who Presides* (New York: Church Publishing, 1995), 15.

4. Transcribed from a recording of a sermon preached by Renee Snead, Columbia Theological Seminary, Decatur, GA, February 27, 2008. Quoted with permission of the author, who is now a Master of Divinity student at Candler School of Theology in Atlanta, GA.

5. Louis-Marie Chauvet, *The Sacraments: The Word of God at the Mercy of the Body* (Collegeville, MN: Liturgical Press, 2001), 114.

6. Church of Scotland, *Common Order* (Edinburgh: St. Andrew Press, 1994), 430.

7. Sarah Coakley, ed., *Religion and the Body* (New York: Cambridge University Press, 1997), 8–9, quoting Thomas P. Kasulis.

8. Samuel Torvend, "Proclaiming and Preaching," in *Ordo: Bath, Word, Prayer, Table; A Liturgical Primer in Honor of Gordon W. Lathrop,* ed. Dirk G. Lange and Dwight W. Vogel (Akron: OSL Publications, 2005), 60.

9. Chauvet, *Sacraments,* 31–32, 34.

10. Sara Miles, *Take This Bread: A Radical Conversion* (New York: Ballantine Books, 2005), 173.

11. Bruce Morrill, *Bodies of Worship: Explorations in Theory and Practice* (Collegeville, MN: Liturgical Press, 1999), 15.

12. Ibid., 6–12.

13. Jane Kenyon, "Cages," in *Collected Poems* (St. Paul, MN: Graywolf Press, 2005), 40.

14. Jeff Smith, *The Frugal Gourmet Keeps the Feast: Past, Present, and Future* (New York: William Morrow & Co., 1995), 3.

15. Ibid., 10.

16. Ike Lee, "The Saving of Soles," in *On Our Way Rejoicing: The 150th Anniversary of Central Presbyterian Church in Atlanta,* ed. Martin Lehfeldt (Atlanta: Central Presbyterian Church, 2007), 140–41.

17. Thank you to Beth Johnson for sharing her story.

18. Nathan Mitchell, *Meeting Mystery: Liturgy, Worship, Sacraments* (Maryknoll, NY: Orbis Books, 2006), 174–75.

19. N. T. Wright, *The Resurrection of the Son of God,* vol. 3 of *Christian Origins and the Question of God* (Minneapolis: Fortress Press, 2003), 289–90, as quoted in Mitchell, *Meeting Mystery,* 180.

20. Augustine, "Your Own Mystery," in *Assembly,* 23:2 (March 1997), accessed online at http://liturgy.nd.edu/assembly/assembly23–2augustine.shtml.

21. Torvend, *Ordo,* 61.

22. Aidan Kavanagh, *Elements of Rite: A Handbook of Liturgical Style* (New York: Pueblo Publishing Co., 1982), 45.

23. Torvend, *Ordo,* 68.

24. Miles, *Take This Bread,* 140.

25. Andrea Bieler and Luise Schottroff, *The Eucharist: Bodies, Bread, and Resurrection* (Minneapolis: Fortress Press, 2007), 127.

26. Ibid., 131.

27. Jeffrey A. Mackey, "Sensing God: The Human Body as a Vehicle of Worship," *The Living Pulpit,* 15:2 (April–June, 2006): 26–27.

28. Mitchell, *Meeting Mystery,* 183, 185–86.

29. Ibid., 180.

30. Kavanagh, *Elements of Rite,* 51–54.

CHAPTER 3: EYES AND EARS

1. Eudora Welty, *One Writer's Beginnings* (Cambridge, MA: Warner Books, 1983), 14.

2. Ibid., 16.

3. Nathan Mitchell, "The Poetics of Space," *Worship* 67.4 (July 1993): 367.

4. Aidan Kavanagh, "Seeing Liturgically," in *Time and Community,* ed. J. Neil Alexander (Washington, DC: The Pastoral Press, 1990), 273.

5. Jim Duffy, "Mae Days," *Chesapeake Life,* November 2008, 106.

6. Annie Dillard, *An American Childhood* (San Francisco: HarperCollins, 1988), 198.

7. Ibid.

8. Thank you to Kathy Wolf for sharing her story.

9. William Seth Adams, *Shaped by Images: One Who Presides* (New York: Church Publishing, 1995), 45–46.

10. Sara Miles, *Take This Bread: A Radical* Conversion (New York: Ballantine Boohs, 2005), 138–39.

11. Adams, *Shaped by Imagdes,* 46.

12. Thomas Merton, *Conjectures of a Guilty Bystander* (New York: Doubleday, 1968), 140–41.

13. Nathan Mitchell, "Being Beautiful, Being Just," in *Toward Ritual Transformation: Remembering Robert W. Hovda,* by Gabe Huck et al. (Collegeville, MN: Liturgical Press, 2003), 73.

14. Elaine Scarry, *On Beauty and Being Just* (Princeton, NJ: Princeton University Press, 1999).

15. Mitchell, "Being Beautiful, Being Just," 74.

16. "Come and Taste," traditional hymn, tune: Farabee, arr. Alice Parker.

17. Don E. Saliers, "Sense, Spirit, and Body in Presiding: A Synaesthetic Environment," *Liturgy* 22, no. 2 (2007): 37.

18. Ibid., 38.

19. Robert W. Hovda, *Strong, Loving, and Wise: Presiding in Liturgy* (Collegeville, MN: Liturgical Press, 1976), 8.

20. Mark R. Francis, *Shape a Circle Ever Wider: Liturgical Inculturation in the United States* (Chicago: Liturgy Training Publications, 2000), 72.

21. Adams, *Shaped by Images,* 47–48.

22. Hovda, *Strong, Loving, and Wise,* 36.

23. Ibid., 17.

24. Ibid., 8

25. Irma S. Rombauer and Marion Rombauer Becker, *The Joy of Cooking,* as quoted in *A Sourcebook about Liturgy,* ed. Gabe Huck (Chicago: Liturgy Training Publications, 1994), 156.

26. Eugenia Gamble, "Among the Ribbons," *Call to Worship: Liturgy, Music, Preaching, and the Arts* 42:3 (February 2009): 45.

27. Saliers, "Sense, Spirit, and Body," 38.

CHAPTER 4: THE MOUTH

1. Mitchell Stephens, *The Rise of the Image, the Fall of the Word* (New York: Oxford University Press, 1998), 5. Neither Stephens nor this author intends this discussion as a tirade against media in worship. Stephens persuasively argues that the invention of video communication is as revolutionary as that of writing or printing. As forms of video communication develop, the church will necessarily continue to consider how media is used effectively and faithfully in worship. Eileen Crowley's work in media as liturgical art is also instructive. See, for instance, her book *A Moving Word: Media Art in Worship* (Minneapolis: Augsburg Fortress, 2006).

2. Richard Lischer, *The End of Words: The Language of Reconciliation in a Culture of Violence,* The Lyman Beecher Lectures in Preaching (Grand Rapids: Wm. B. Eerdmans Publishing Co., 2005), 13.

3. Ibid., 24.

4. Ibid., 26.

5. Kathleen Norris, "Words and the Word: Poet on Pilgrimage," *Christian Century*, April 16, 1997, 381.

6. Ibid.

7. Ibid.

8. Stephen H. Webb, *The Divine Voice: Christian Proclamation and the Theology of Sound* (Grand Rapids: Brazos Press, 2004), 32.

9. Ibid., 14.

10. Ibid., 15.

11. Ibid., 49.

12. See ibid., 51–55, for his own discussion of this matter. See also Kathy Black, *A Healing Homiletic: Preaching and Disability* (Nashville: Abingdon Press, 1996), for helpful discussion of biblical texts dealing with deafness, and guidance for preaching from those texts with sensitivity to the deaf community.

13. George Herbert, *Herbert's Poems and Country Parson, A New Edition; with a Life of the Author from Isaac Walton* (London: Haynes & Son, 1826, photocopied edition), 70, as quoted in Thomas H. Troeger, "A House of Prayer in the Heart: How Homiletics Nurtures the Church's Spirituality," *Call to Worship: Liturgy, Music, Preaching, and the Arts* 40.3 (2007): 2.

14. Troeger, "A House of Prayer," 2–3.

15. Ibid., 6.

16. See Thomas G. Long, *The Witness of Preaching*, 2nd ed. (Louisville, KY: Westminster John Knox Press, 2005), 45ff., for a discussion of preaching as bearing witness.

17. Thomas A. Kane, *The Dancing Church around the World* (Tomaso Production: 2004).

18. Leanne van Dyk, ed., *A More Profound Alleluia: Theology and Worship in Harmony* (Grand Rapids: Wm. B. Eerdmans Publishing Co., 2004), 71–72.

19. Karl Barth, *Church Dogmatics,* vol. I/1, trans. G. T. Thomson and Harold Knight (Edinburgh: T&T Clark, 1956), 106.

20. Patrick Willson, "Shouting the Whisper: The Sacrament of the Word," *Call to Worship: Liturgy, Music, Preaching, and the Arts* 40.4 (2007): 4.

21. Bishops' Committee on Priestly Life and Ministry, *Fulfilled in Your Hearing: The Homily in the Sunday Assembly* (Washington, DC: U.S. Conference of Catholic Bishops, 1982), 41.

22. William Hill, "Preaching as a 'Moment' in Theology," in *Search for the Absent God* (New York: Crossroad Publishing, 1992), 186, as quoted in Paul A. Janowiak, SJ, "Preaching as the Presence of Christ: The Word within the Word," *Call to Worship: Liturgy, Music, Preaching, and the Arts* 40.4 (2007): 13.

23. Willson, "Shouting the Whisper," 7.

24. Webb, *The Divine Voice,* 209.

25. Ibid., 210.

26. See, for example, Jana Childers, *Performing the Word* (Nashville: Abingdon Press, 1998); and Richard F. Ward, *Speaking of the Holy: The Art of Communication in Preaching* (St. Louis: Chalice Press, 2001).

27. James Mays, *Psalms* (Louisville, KY: John Knox Press, 1994), 201.

28. Dietrich Bonhoeffer, *Life Together* (New York: Harper & Row, 1954), 110.

29. Frederick Buechner, *Whistling in the Dark: An ABC Theologized* (San Francisco: Harper & Row, 1988), 55–56.

30. Emily Brink, "Make Me a Blessing," *Reformed Worship* 19 (March 1991): 2.

31. This version, from the *Book of Common Worship* (Louisville, KY: Westminster/John Knox Press, 1993), alters verse 25, "The LORD make his face to shine upon you, and be gracious to you" (NRSV).

32. Patrick D. Miller Jr., "The Blessing of God: An Interpretation of Numbers 6:22–27," *Interpretation* 29 (July 1975): 244–47.

33. Ibid., 246.

34. Paul Pruyser, "The Master Hand: Psychological Notes on Pastoral Blessing," in *The New Shape of Pastoral Theology*, ed. William B. Oglesby Jr. (Nashville: Abingdon Press, 1969), 358.

35. Carolyn Gratton, *Trusting* (New York: Crossroad, 1982), 210, as quoted in John S. Mogabgab, "Editor's Introduction," *Weavings* 5, no. 5 (September/October 1990): 3.

36. Harold Fickett and Douglas R. Gilbert, *Flannery O'Connor: Images of Grace* (Grand Rapids: Wm. B. Eerdmans Publishing Co., 1986), 38.

37. Colbert S. Cartwright and O. I. Cricket Harrison, compilers and eds., *Chalice Worship* (St. Louis: Chalice Press, 1997), 437.

38. Ibid., 440.

39. Miller, "The Blessing of God," 249.

40. Thanks to the Rev. Gary Charles for this felicitous phrase.

41. Miller, "The Blessing of God," 250.

42. Don E. Saliers, *Worship and Spirituality*, 2nd ed. (Akron: OSL Publications, 1996), 29.

43. Jonathan Yardley, "The Writer Who Was Full of Grace," *Washington Post,* sec. C, July 6, 2005.

44. Pruyser, "The Master Hand," 361.

45. Ibid., 357.

46. Marilynne Robinson, *Gilead: A Novel* (New York: Macmillan Publishing Co., 2004), 241.

47. Lischer, *The End of Words,* 26.

48. Catherine Madsen, "Love Songs to the Dead: The Liturgical Voice as Mentor and Reminder," *CrossCurrents* 41.4 (Winter 1998–99): 4.

49. Catherine Madsen, "The Common Word: Recovering Liturgical Speech," CrossCurrents 52.2 (Summer 2002): 234–36.

50. T. S. Eliot, "The Use of Poetry," as quoted in Craig Raine, *T. S. Eliot* (New York: Oxford University Press, 2006), 142.

51. Gail Ramshaw, *Worship: Searching for Language* (Washington, DC: The Pastoral Press, 1988), 111.

52. Ibid., 112–13.

53. Norris, "Words and the Word," 381.

54. *Book of Common Worship*, 53.

55. Annie Dillard, *Holy the Firm,* rev. ed. (New York: Harper & Row, 1988), 59.

56. Gail Ramshaw, *Reviving Sacred Speech: The Meaning of Liturgical Language, Second Thoughts on Christ in Sacred Speech* (Akron, OH: OSL Publications, 2000), 3–4.

57. Kathleen Norris, "Drawing on Metaphor," *Christian Century,* September 24–October 1, 1997, 842.

58. Evangelical Lutheran Church in America, *Principles for Worship* (Minneapolis: Augsburg Fortress, 2002), 15.

59. Gilbert Ostdiek, "Crafting English Prayer Texts: The ICEL Revision of the Sacramentary," *Studia liturgica* 26 (1996): 131–32.

60. Norris, "Drawing on Metaphor," 842.

61. Ibid.

62. International Commission on English in the Liturgy, *Opening Prayers: Collects in Contemporary Language, Scripture-related Prayers for Sundays and Holy Days, Years A, B, and C* (Norwich, CT: Canterbury Press, 2001), 98.

63. See Childers, *Performing the Word,* 57–77, for a thorough introduction to voice production for preachers and presiders.

64. Siobhán Garrigan, "The Spirituality of Presiding," *Liturgy* 22:2 (2007): 4.

65. Ibid., 5.

CHAPTER 5: THE HANDS

1. This story was told by John McCain on the National Public Radio series "I Believe," broadcast on October 17, 2005.

2. Romano Guardini, *Sacred Signs*, revised and introduced by Melissa Kay (Wilmington, DE: Michael Glazier, 1979), 18, as quoted in Nathan Mitchell, "Toward a Poetics of Gesture," *Worship* 75, no. 4 (July 2001): 360.

3. For a more detailed explanation of the history and meaning of this posture, see Elochukwu E. Uzukwu, *Worship as Body Language: Introduction to Christian Worship; An African Orientation* (Collegeville, MN: Liturgical Press, 1997, 20–21.

4. Patrick Malloy, *Celebrating the Eucharist: A Practical Ceremonial Guide for Clergy and Other Liturgical Ministers* (New York: Church Publishing, 2007), 102.

5. Craig A. Satterlee, *Presiding in the Assembly* (Minneapolis: Augsburg Fortress, 2003), 18.

6. Aidan Kavanagh comments: "If a poet must explain the poem before it is recited, there is something wrong with the poem. If a liturgy must be explained before it is done, there is something wrong with the liturgy. . . . This is not to say that preparation is never needed. It is only to say that lengthy explanations are always abnormal and should never occur as an immediate prelude to the act itself. The assembly needs sustained preparation and formation of various sorts—evangelical, homiletical, catechetical, and ascetical. It is when these are lacking that last-minute recourse is had on the part of slothful ministers to verbose explanations of what is about to happen. The risk this runs is that of turning the liturgy into a 'learning experience,' as it is called. In a culture such as ours, the educational temptation is difficult to resist. But liturgy which is stylish and effective in incrementing *logos* leads not to the brink of clarity but to the edge of chaos. It deals not with the abolition of ambiguity but with the dark and hidden things of God. When it comes to liturgy, precision can be bought at too high a price, and some things cannot be said." From his *Elements of Rite: A Handbook of Liturgical Style* (New York: Pueblo Publishing Co., 1982), 101–2.

7. Mark Searle, "Bowing," *Assembly* 6:3 (1979): 79, as quoted in Kathleen Hughes, R.S.C.J., *Lay Presiding: The Art of Leading Prayer* (Collegeville, MN: Liturgical Press, 1988), 25–26.

8. John Calvin, *Institutes of the Christian Religion*, 4.17.1; ed. John T. McNeill, trans. Ford Lewis Battles, 2 vols., LCC (Philadelphia: Westminster Press, 1960), 2:1361.

9. Ibid., 4.17.43, in 2:1420.

10. From Thanksgiving over the Water, option 1, *Book of Common Worship* (Louisville, KY: Westminster/John Knox Press, 1993), 411.

11. A Prayer of Thanksgiving, Supplication, and Intercession in the *Book of Common Worship* contains these words: "Especially we thank you for your servant *N.,* whose baptism is now complete in death" (p. 921). If we are baptized into Christ's life and death, we are also baptized into his resurrection; therefore what was begun in our water baptism is completed in our dying and rising in Christ.

12. Gail Ramshaw, "Water," in *Treasures Old and New: Images in the Lectionary* (Minneapolis: Fortress Press, 2002), 409.

13. Kathleen Hughes, *Lay Presiding: The Art of Leading Prayer* (Collegeville, MN: Liturgical Press, 1988), 15.

14. Ben Ratliff, "He May Have Left His Heart, but He Brought His Hands," *New York Times*, December 18, 2008. Accessed at http://www.nytimes.com/2008/12/18/arts/music/18benn.html.

15. Gabe Huck and Gerald T. Chinchar, *Liturgy with Style and Grace* (Chicago: Liturgy Training Publications, 1998), 46.

16. Archdiocese of Chicago, *This Is the Night: A Parish Welcomes New Catholics* (Chicago: Liturgy Training Publications, 1992).

17. Kavanagh, *Elements of Rite*, 54.

18. Jerry L. Van Marter, "Tlingit Matriarchs Present 'Healing Robe' to Alaska Presbytery," Presbyterian News Service, accessed on line at http://www.pcusa.org/pcnews/2008/08799.htm. A photograph of the robe is included in the article.

19. See, for example, *Book of Common Worship*, p. 413: "O Lord, uphold *N.* by your Holy Spirit. Give *him/her* the spirit of wisdom and understanding, the spirit of counsel and might, the spirit of knowledge and the fear of the Lord, the spirit of joy in your presence, both now and forever." This is a version of an ancient prayer that is used by a number of denominations.

20. The separation of baptism and confirmation is a complex question that goes beyond the bounds of this work. For a thorough discussion see Maxwell E. Johnson, *The Rites of Christian Initiation: Their Evolution and Interpretation*, revised and expanded edition (Collegeville, MN: Liturgical Press, 2007).

21. Sara Miles, *Take This Bread: A Radical Conversion* (New York: Ballantine Books, 2005), 156–57.

22. Don E. Saliers, "Toward a Spirituality of Inclusiveness," in *Human Disability and the Service of God: Reassessing Religious Practice*, ed. Nancy L. Eiesland and Don E. Saliers (Nashville: Abingdon Press, 1998), 19–20.

23. Tertullian, *De resurrectione mortuorum* 8.2–3, as quoted in Nathan Mitchell, "The Poetics of Space," *Worship* 67, no. 4 (July 1993): 364.

CHAPTER 6: THE FEET

1. Gertrud Mueller Nelson, "Christian Formation of Children: The Role of Ritual and Celebration," in *Liturgy and Spirituality in Context: Perspectives on Prayer and Culture,* ed. Eleanor Bernstein, CSI, as quoted in *A Sourcebook about Liturgy,* ed. Gabe Huck (Chicago: Liturgy Training Publications, 1994), 67.

2. Nathan Mitchell, *Meeting Mystery* (Maryknoll, NY: Orbis Books, 2006), 51.

3. Ibid., 59.

4. Thomas A. Kane, *The Dancing Church around the World* (DVD), Tomaso Production, 2004. Kane notes that at liturgies during other times of the year, the clay pot symbolizes a seed that holds the Word.

5. Mitchell, *Meeting Mystery,* 183.

6. "What Is This Place?" Text by Huub Oosterhuis, trans. David Smith, in *Evangelical Lutheran Worship* (Minneapolis: Augsburg Fortress, 2006), 524.

7. William Seth Adams, *Moving the Furniture: Liturgical Theory, Practice, and Environment* (New York: Church Publishing, 1999), 141.

8. Robin Jensen, *The Substance of Things Seen: Art, Faith, and the Christian Community* (Grand Rapids: Wm. B. Eerdmans Publishing Co., 2004), 109.

9. To read Chauvet's compelling thoughts on the matter, see his "The Liturgy in its Symbolic Space," in *Liturgy and the Body,* ed. Louis Chauvet and François Kabasek Lumbala (London: SCM Press; Maryknoll, NY: Orbis Books, 1995), 36.

10. For a more thorough discussion of liturgical spaces and liturgical centers, see James F. White, *Introduction to Christian Worship*, 3rd ed. (Nashville: Abingdon Press, 2000), 86–103.

11. *Invitation to Christ: Font and Table* (Presbyterian Church (U.S.A.), 2006) is an example of one denomination's attempt to encourage congregations to reclaim the centrality of the sacraments in worship. Five simple practices are commended, including to "lead appropriate parts of weekly worship from the font and from the table."

12. John Calvin, *Institutes of the Christian Religion* 4.14.17; ed. John T. McNeill, trans. Ford Lewis Battles, 2 vols. (Philadelphia: Westminster Press, 1960), 2:1292.

13. In some traditions baptismal space is more like a pool than a basin. Thanks be to God for that! These remarks are directed toward presiders who serve in congregations with fonts. The suggestions offered here might be adapted for use in sanctuaries that have baptismal pools at the level of the congregation. More thinking must be done around how these ideas translate into spaces where baptisms take place in an elevated baptistry.

14. *Book of Common Worship* (Louisville, KY: Westminster/John Knox Press, 1993), 473.

15. Ibid., 56.

16. Marney A. Wasserman, "Leading from Font, Table, and Pulpit," *Call to Worship: Liturgy, Music, Preaching, and the Arts* 40.4 (2007): 19.

17. *Book of Common Worship*, 159–60.

18. Wasserman, "Leading," 19.

19. Ibid.

20. For instance, the congregation might sing one of the "shorter songs for worship" published by the Iona Community: "Jesus Christ, Jesus Christ, Son of God among us, Thank you for every sign showing that you love us." The song may be repeated until the action is complete. See "Jesus Christ, Jesus Christ," words and music by John Bell, in *There Is One Among Us: Shorter Songs for Worship,* ed. John Bell (Chicago: GIA Publications, 1998), 38–39.

21. The conviction of this author, and of a growing number of Christians in Protestant circles, is that Word and Table are two parts of a whole and should not be separated. Certainly Anglican and Lutheran traditions have inherited the practice, and John Calvin was a proponent of weekly Communion. The story of how Word and Table became separated is complex and multifaceted. In recent years, however, a number of faith communities have recognized the need for the gospel to be proclaimed in Word *and* in Sacrament. As the ecumenical convergence around this question continues, we may well see more churches move toward weekly Eucharist. Nevertheless, it is important not to dismiss those traditions for whom this is not a priority.

22. One caveat, of course: at pulpit, font, and table we pray for the illumining, empowering action of the Holy Spirit. Prayers for illumination, prayers of thanksgiving over the water, and prayers of thanksgiving at the table all contain an epiclesis.

23. Wasserman, "Leading," 22.

24. Psalm 24:1, *Book of Common Worship*, 67.

25. See, for example, the prayers on pages 158 and 159 of the *Book of Common Worship*.

26. Mitchell, *Meeting Mystery,* 180.

27. Ibid., 38.

28. Don E. Saliers, *Worship as Theology: Foretaste of Glory Divine* (Nashville: Abingdon Press, 1994), 49.

CHAPTER 7: THE HEART

1. Raymond Van Leeuwen, "The Book of Proverbs," *The New Interpreter's Bible,* vol. 5 (Nashville: Abingdon Press, 1997), 60.

2. Thank you to Christine Yoder for this insight.

3. Gordon W. Lathrop, *The Pastor: A Spirituality* (Minneapolis: Fortress Press, 2006), 25.

4. Ibid.

5. *Book of Common Worship* (Louisville, KY: Westminster/John Knox Press, 1993), 57.

6. Aidan Kavanagh, *Elements of Rite: A Handbook of Liturgical Style* (New York: Pueblo Publishing Co., 1982), 13.

7. Robert D. McFadden, "All-Embracing Man of Action for a New Era of Papacy," *New York Times,* April 3, 2005; accessed online at http://www.nytimes.com/2005/04/03/international/europe/03pope.html.

8. Craig A. Satterlee, *Presiding in the Assembly* (Minneapolis: Augsburg Fortress, 2003), 20.

9. Kathleen Hughes, *Lay Presiding: The Art of Leading Prayer* (Collegeville, MN: Liturgical Press, 1988), 13.

10. Robert Hovda, as quoted in Gabe Huck and Gerald T. Chinchar, *Liturgy with Style and Grace* (Chicago: Liturgy Training Publications, 1998), 47.

11. John Calvin, *Institutes of the Christian Religion* 4.14.8; ed. John T. McNeill, trans. Ford Lewis Battles, 2 vols., LCC (Philadelphia: Westminster Press, 1960), 2:1284.

12. I am, of course, a huge fan of playacting, just not by ministers in church.

13. Annie Dillard, *Teaching a Stone to Talk: Expeditions and Encounters* (New York: Harper & Row, 1982), 20.

14. Robert Hovda, *Strong, Loving, and Wise* (Collegeville, MN: Liturgical Press, 1976), 13.